Works MMXXIV: Prohibition, Kosmokrator, Borges

Yperion Library, Volume 1

YPERION

Published by Yperion Press, 2024.

While every precaution has been taken in the preparation of this book, the publisher assumes no responsibility for errors or omissions, or for damages resulting from the use of the information contained herein.

WORKS MMXXIV: PROHIBITION, KOSMOKRATOR, BORGES

First edition. October 21, 2024.

Copyright © 2024 YPERION.

ISBN: 979-8227262523

Written by YPERION.

Table of Contents

PROHIBITION 1
KOSMOKRATOR 117
Primary Practices 119
The Practice, not the Philosophy 125
Why NOT Lucid Dreaming and Astral Projection? ... 129
Remote Viewing for Stabilizing the Artist's State of Flow 133
Journal—Intensely 137
Walking the Tightrope 141
"It don't matter what you believe" 147
Trusting Sensations 151
Just Enough 157
World Domination 159
BORGES 163
Prologue 165
The artist's work is one 167
On being ruled 171
An unbearably sentimental man 175
Transforming experience into symbol 179
Erring to learn 183
A book is already too much 187
Once something is written 191
The spoken word 195
A barrier between writer and reader 199
I don't try to please anyone 203
On realizing his destiny 207
I read what I enjoy 211
On writing well 215
On death 221
On learning a language 225
The natural, the organic 229

To Elytron Frass, for his continued support, advice, and contrapunctal commentary.

And to the Evil that led to the creation of Yperion Press.

Foreword

This collection is comprised of three works. The first one, *Prohibition*, was the result of psychological self-torture and the application of reason-evasive techniques, or so the author thought. The idea was to overload and distract and shock the mind with texts and ideas disagreeable to the author, and to then synthesize a winning strategy through and over them. The result was the novella. Two subsequent episodes were originally planned and sketched.

The second of the three works is *Kosmokrator*. Originally intended as the first issue in a series of journals exploring the out-of-body experience and expanded perception, it grew to become a sequence of essays on mental health and independent thinking. Whether the series of journals will continue is yet to be seen.

The third work is titled *Borges*, after Jorge Luis Borges, the Argentinean fantasy story writer, poet, and essayist. This short book intends to explore the Borges' thought and attitudes from an often transcribed but seldom discussed angle: his interviews and other oral presentations. The author of the present volume is of the opinion that this is the richest and deepest facet of Borges as a human.

PROHIBITION

A surrealist castigation novel

Spread across the fortress, visual recording machinery and audio sensors never sleep. Some few among us have mastered the art of evading these. But I now harbor a secret conviction. The governess, so I held to be true, possesses far more mysterious means of surveillance. That or we fail to detect more advanced technological contraptions.

Machinery devised by the engineering division escapes the imaginations of most of us, something beyond the insidious affair of organic networks of information and disinformation, something that for us signifies a terrible blow to rebellious aspirations, an extension of her programming whispers hissing words in our ears, it tells us that those above must be telling the truth.

Her control is so complete that there is no point in second-guessing her. Whenever her emissaries unveil her designs, we must take them at face value. They are a rendition of her plans curated especially for our ears, her messages ooze with honey, her approach surpasses the brute force associated with great dictatorships. Her dialectic is an invitation into cavernous regions, underground kingdoms, flame-lit and stone-carved temples. Only the initiated tread those hallowed steps.

Her sensual lips float above the rushing waterfall, unspoken words come crashing over our heads, they form a curtain between the world out there and the imagined world inside. Smoke irradiates from the engines around and throughout the facility. Here, where no sign of greenery grows.

Massive black mirrors set atop marble plinths compensate for the technological excess. But the *how* of it, to be precise, I ignore. It is something felt, not thought nor spoken. It gives the illusion of depth and space that do not exist. And yet, through some unfair trickery, they open up spaces within you more real than anything else. Nothing could ever hope to be as real as that which funnels your dreams into her vortex.

Like a reverse dawn that creeps and ruptures through the memories of mothers and fathers that gave us away, willingly or otherwise, her glowing and untrustworthy presence makes itself felt in the most unexpected of moments. If ignored, her deafening cries will drive the most reticent or uncooperative elements to bend to her will in the course of the pattern of delivery for which a different actor is responsible. While we must remain well within the limits of valor and virtue when dealing with the humans that exist outside the premises, the process of compensation demands that we in turn bear the full burden of violence without the slightest hint of reactionary tremor.

Deprived and mutilated, I was allowed to continue my functions. Active, even overt, surveillance was upon me. A bionic arm, a jewel from the werewolf throne, my legacy from that rueful day. The arm I lost in giving my all to free my stiff member from the grip, the grip of an ape I held down and sought to apply iron hand techniques to breaking its forearm. It, in turn, pulled at my arm, tearing it from its socket. The jewel, a different story.

The kindness we show our newest prisoner has its limits. There will come a time when, given the continued disavowal of those social courtesies we extend to him, the friendly slaps and slight bruising must give way to more sophisticated methods of persuasion.

As he clings wordless to his smiling convictions, a part of him crumbles. Whether that is faith in our distant humanity or his own loyalty to humankind lying without our walls, whence he came reluctantly, is not something I feel I can answer with full conviction. Ask yourself whether you'd let such a poignant, penetrating thrust, plant the seed of doubt within your deepest self.

Sometimes, a different kind of violence, an affront that changes the frame, leads to power. Even in apparent defeat, you may be rewarded. The struggle to keep intact my sanctum sanctorum must have moved her. No, I lie to you, and I lie to myself. The severity of my actions, my sacrifice in the service of our most potent energy projector, *those* were indicators to her.

The officer turned giant werewolf, now held in a cell. The sacrificed Valkyrie, too sweet a fruit of Eden for command, clasped by silver chains. They became subjects of experiment once some inscrutable judgment drove them here. And yet, I am drawn to these individuals.

I contemplated them with mixed feelings of admiration and mystifying longing. Your friends may continue to remember you forever, someone like you. I lack that luxury, and you take it for granted. You took it for granted until our goddess ambushed you, you who should have been ever ready. In that, I have bested you. And yet, in doing so, I was not ripped away from the womb of our chain of command. You are now both different beings, battered but free in a way the rest of us can never hope to be again.

You will remain ignorant until you place everything under the full light of our alien space. Until then, you will not have begun to understand the full extent of power. To understand the power that links with great operations. Power infusing with an uncontrollable rage simmering under the surface of your features. Powers that allow forces success in their conquering of your body. They fracture your mind into separate personality clusters.

Abducted, he says to me. And the inexplicable grief when personal photographs slide before me feels too distant. His original response styles were very different, much too different. For now, it suffices to realize that force and violence never were the keys. The werewolf could not talk. Being one of the few outside the inner circle to wield the power of telepathy, I received this assignment.

Possible victory existed within our means. They would have been ours had the courage and energy necessary been present. We should have known we needed to continue striving longer along a path laid down with ruses. Empathy flourishes. The more a friendship flourishes, the more I understand. The more I reveal, the less I need him to speak. The more I learn, the less I am given to report to the governess.

And yet, how do you hide your thoughts from someone who can read them?

Seated upon her invisible throne of delights, the mother of all wrongs never sleeps. She blinds us with the brilliance of her desire for power. It is a combination of accurate calculation and elaborate maneuvers. Would that I could, lay these mortal eyes upon her hallowed countenance once more. Would that I could, watch her alabaster feet descend dove-like upon the steel plates of the citadel.

Those two stars that I dream of as her eyes would see within me, taking me inside her and allaying her need for secrecy. So dreams the dutiful servant that I am. But the theologian in me knows better. Better than to insist on divinity to visit me in the flesh. For that would break me into shards of terror.

My eyes also turned inward, for in me, too, were a Valkyrie and a werewolf. That I had to find a way to get them out was not in doubt. That access to them had landed on my lap without justification sounded a clear warning. A warning, yes, and a taunting. *What shalt thou do now, vermin?*

He wants to maintain his loyalty, this stranger. But in this life, I speak only to you, I say to him. He is not quick to accept authority, yet at the same time he is eager to please. I let him know in strange sentences that I am aware of this, of his tendency. I do so, that he may see me as the familiar land he seeks immersed in a lake of despair.

Inasmuch as he is disloyal, I must make him demonstrate loyalty in tangible ways. The moment will come when I may turn that impulse to our benefit, the long-awaited spring. I telephone for someone to come in to act as legal counsel. This person serves only the function of a witness.

The subject is a gush of water, trembling at the first sight of something new. After he spends some time with him, the legal counsel takes his papers and walks into an inner office. I, the questioner, emerge having given instructions to the guard. Take the subject back to his small cell, to his sweet darkness. Let him know, state it clear and loud, that we do not need him any longer.

His body becomes a striving delight, he cries for the one left behind. A girl, the lonely girl of his past. Whatever pattern he has chosen in life he takes for his destiny within the cultural milieu. The paradox, of course, is that any destiny is a choice. And we would yet make a martyr, or worse still, a priest, out of this whimpering revolutionary. The present perception of reality as a frozen image stands corrected.

The dynamic mutations upon which humanity thrives become evident when standing outside. Outside in the void. Located outside of everything. Behind everything. Below everything.

Whenever succor escapes out of reach, as it is for me nightly, I have one choice alone. To either march out that very moment or stay put with your facile speech. One feels the need to be independent, to display initiative, even as any of them may drive you mad.

As I ponder these things in my own cold cell, another problem area comes into proper perspective. Distortions occur between the message we intend and what the masses perceive. We can them all back to the imperfection of the out-of-body coincidence.

We cannot, in truth, lie to them. Individuals with high brain activity tend to become aggressive. The only palliative is true soothing emotion. Those with less drive remain dormant, only fleeting paranoids. These last are not at all uncommon.

On the metallic slate I have come to call my bed, sudden realizations reemerge. Ripening fruits growing in the depths of awareness speak only to me. Roots are absent and, in their stead, gardens of gaudy spring answer your real mouth. Hidden from view.

The awareness of a never-inert matter, awareness of ourselves as a part of its permanent motion, awareness of such a motion in a perpetual interaction with itself. We are the elevation of its manifestation in the explicit form of the physical. After an hour, I rise again, emerging into the outer office to ask for a statement. And I realize that not even the gold of these pages is real.

The high domed ceiling of the vault below ground contains the great black werewolf. On a gray stone seat he sits, chained, collar of arcane gem discs still around his throat. He snarls, eyes full of fear. They tell me that of plans to breed the beast with the fallen handmaiden. The evasive leadership is aware she might be carrying the progeny of the file and rank. That was a punishment she took on herself. It appears we must wait for a season.

The overseer enters the metallic scene. Her skin, blue, her eyes blanked out. A tall crown upon her head reminiscent of ancient Egypt. Its black color, glossy surface, and shape betrays a colder, more alien design. She is part of a harsh matriarchy that long ago overthrew male domination.

To curtail the downsides of female rule, they adopted a phallic worship. An overt and depersonalized cult. The underlying drive ties in a secret methodology. The dominating matron, at the behest of the courtesan, gives a place for males to excel. But always under her divine intervention.

In contrast to the older, weaker tendency, the weaker males die by the hand of a female assassin. The all-female guild is in charge of children during their first six years. The phallic matriarchy adopts the wordless and sensuous cold power of the female. It marries it to the raging decisiveness and nostalgia of the male. The best of both worlds according to the words of the governess.

The werewolf, thus, is but an instrument to strengthen the matron's line. Its savagery tested; its original genetic composition developed through harsh conditions. A soldier, an officer, and a beast through trans-dimensional possession.

The exhausted immigrant shows his frail beauty. The nature of his compensation is all too obvious to me. He is much more primitive than anyone wants to admit. For fear of opposing orders from above, no doubt. His uniqueness comes in the form of a kind of mist-clothed high magic.

This total stranger has proven himself capable of escaping detection. Both personnel and specialized interrogators have done nothing but exacerbate his hate. I will uncover him by letting him become himself once again. I will give him the chance to become consumed by emotion, blinded by confusion. To this end, the architects designed the facility.

Security considerations, block planning, interrogation rooms, considerations beyond. They thought of everything, especially the training of facility personnel and internal guards. The whole purpose of this machinery of concrete, steel and flesh is to wield cruelty. Its aim is to take away all that seems real to the subject and place it within view but out of reach. At first, that is.

Later on, the familiar becomes, through intelligent design, unreliable, cumbersome. And the bizarre, in turn, begins to feel commonplace. All is necromantic reference. Every single pound of flesh is then considered. Each morsel weighed on the scales of experimentation.

His mouth will remember the flavor of fists. He will learn to respect the privilege of freedom. He becomes a spiritual look-alike with all the rest of those who came before him. Only in his becoming a deathless cry, sustaining an adamant glare, will he be free again. A reasoning mind behind all personality traits will I allow him to join us. I stand on the threshold. I am the watcher. But please realize that I am kind.

Experience indicates that all it takes is for the message to bury into his flesh. Then, and only then, physical violence need not occur. In fact, the organization would prefer it if potential agents were not mutilated. The goal of the wise is to shape them, to show them an ocean of possibilities. In its depths, they see themselves as solitary particles, flying into the unknown.

To convince them that this state of unknowns is a costly challenge. This peace in the midst of folly is the only way to allow their wings to spread and lift them into the wintry sky. The price paid in hefty bags of gold pays its dividends.

As strength begins to fail, all subsequent efforts lose their power to damage. External behavior translates into symbols in the subject's mind. They induce thought, action and speech as needed of him. And this comes as a willingness, subjugation to a higher mind, an inner mind.

The giant paw, the bloody claw, now limp, the chemical sleeplessness. They keep my voice in his head. Outside, an orange light falling on the courtyard. Outside, the sprawling tree branches bearing decapitated human heads. They sway in the wind, audible branch rustling, and his yellow eyes follow, staring and humid.

We accept the inability of the universe to provide consistency. We accept also the myriad changes which come as a matter of course. This is what we all prefer.

Elsewhere, an accomplice, a runaway slave of the lycanthrope cult.

She was here, too. Deepening the mystery, the labyrinth of knowledge, with each step she took. Her skin was the pale of death, and her limbs and organs were ever ready for stimulation. Total awareness, she was. Most evolved, she was most in touch with her primitive orientations. She diverged from those of us who still clung to our unique and basic adjustment. She was beyond personality, she was present, she had power, and she enjoyed it all.

I saw her extend a terrible arm towards our unwilling visitor. I know your name, said she. And he quivered under her gaze. Naked, his hand clung to a hairless skull, courtesy of our welcoming ministrations. You are more like us than you realize, and you would do well to reveal what you know to us. Her sympathetic voice dispelled confusion.

Injustice and cruelty are furthest from our minds, she said to him. But tearing you apart as your terrible cries fill these vast and lonely halls will only be a death you welcome. We know of your cult of night, cult of Dionysus, of your religious self-offer to a horrifying death. Such wishes shall not come true here. Not if they were to afford you any manner of satisfaction.

The gray of her hair attested only to her dramatic aesthetic choice. For while the huntress had outlived generations of mortals, her physiology was divine. Alien it was, too, at once alluring and terrorizing.

Cumbersome were our prejudices when standing before the real. The weight and unmanageability of thoughts affected the lines upon our faces. Ours were decaying bodies aching for transformation. We, awaiting, growing in stellar infusions of light. We yearned to flicker in and out of the asphyxiating confines of this familiar landscape.

She floated above the floor and a finger she placed on the curled body of the candidate. The gentle action causing him to scream out in pain was telling. Telling of occult power and intentions. The cluster of personalities to which he belonged shared his eternal behavior.

The skill of the questioner lies in distinguishing between these cloned souls. Understanding what would draw him out, open up, collaborate, and, in his case, ascend to our position. The path of the nightmare, the path of the machine. Ours are dead eyes that see no future but only an eternal sequence of presents.

Her yellow eyes, blisters above the same mouth that kissed and sucked. Indulgent in plain acts of carnal abandon, she was now ready to bite and tear her prey apart. A swift kick broke the trance, and we heard his ribs crack under the tremendous force of her naked foot. Take him away.

I avoided thinking to myself that this was poor form; lacking technique. The damage incurred affected the effectiveness of future attempts. The collection of approaches that could be viable diminished. Force is not necessary. She might have heard my neural implants racing. I knew better than to allow them to form into recognizable patterns. This much I knew how to do well.

An infernal facility, a gospel of security. Grand contributions to the growth of humankind. They all say upon the threshold of morality. Not only did we sanction the cruel trespass by our silence, but we did nothing to relieve his pain.

Why, you could ask. The reasons are complex and many to enumerate here. Let me assure you neither cowardice nor blind obedience have anything to do with it. There is an ideal point in the administration of wanton violence. As deplorable as it might seem to you, a point where horrendous pain transforms and realigns the self.

I placed him in a heated room, support built into his torso, nutrients infused. No palliative succored his troubled mind. But I sat with him there. All the times I had united with the authoress of this cruelty came to mind. Penetrating her arching body, head tilted back, our consciousnesses united. Actions like these felt alien to those moments, my weaker side pronounced. But they are two sides of the same coin, said the deeper voice within me.

She is in touch with the hungry beast inside her. In balance with the machine, she is outside, making her take greater strides. Unlike you, who wallow in insignificance. You are good enough only for moments of distraction. For these menial tasks that required mere intellect and rationale.

Without prompting, he began to speak to me, a stream of words uncontrolled. Words hued violet in my mind, for all such things framed so came to me in this vibrancy, such a particular one. Yet he did not deliver what the huntress had expected. She, the goddess who hunts my waking dreams, my relay to the governess.

He spoke of the world outside. He spoke of golden pollen flowers white. Also, of memories crystalline and dappled with spirits of the air, with sprinklings of mud. He filled my mind with his imagination, creating an archway between him and me. It was a curved path, not a straight one that would have been too much to bear for me.

Perhaps he knew that.

Had he taken pity upon me even from the precarious condition entrapping his being? This mere mortal upon whom we looked down on and even pitied knew something the rest of us ignored...

It hinted at something that was not known or experienced. It was created in the synthesis of minds. Thus was I entranced in unexpected commerce with the prisoner. And then something shook my body.

It was not the fabled mystic experience as I considered for one moment in disgust. It was the ungrateful cretin who tried his luck. By attacking me he had forfeited his life. With a pair of cables, he had wrenched from the wall I ended his life. A pair of cables, still conducting electricity. He had shown me enough to want to know more.

As much as I had grown to long for the cold embrace, I suspected a different world. The pleasures of the totalitarian physical control of the mind had their allure. Beyond the mental control of the body, there was something more.

The world given to us is not the world we want, those of us born a different breed. We sense we must make a run for it, reach for and grasp the shades beyond the veil. And by this sentiment, felt I, would I rise or fall. Enthrone myself or fall into the bottomless abyss of unknowing.

His death was necessary for me to capture that destiny. Not only because my revenge had to close this cycle, but because the laws of the universe so dictated. Having gone off track with the strictest protocols, I decided to seize the day.

As I joined my alien lover in dark and eternal congress a transformation occurred. My dark flesh and her impossible whiteness fused. Our linked consciousnesses battled for supremacy. We hung from the tree of forbidden knowledge.

The exhaust fumes rising from the vents below served as the screen. It received and amplified our projections. On this battlefield I defeated her. My thoughts implanted deep within her. Such accursed operations, in the end, caused my flesh and programming to morph irreversibly.

We trained a stoic outlook. It was a mimicry of lower spheres. They were authentic insofar as they remained unchanged. Unchanged by the little events that surround them. We thought that by such an approach we could, in time, come closer to the grand stellar beings of the cosmos.

Friendly, we should avoid drifting into anything foreign to our will and desire for too long a time. To live with stability, the conflict of personalities remains necessary. Struggle keeps things in check. Where self-esteem hurries outside, all involved subjects come to feel the weight of it all. The weight of reality. The weight of that which cares not how you feel. So does balance come into view, through strict discipline. Through staring into the face of *want* and *rejection*.

Hostility from the deepest recesses fills our erectness here in this room. Our subjectivity is best handled with a calm interest. It is best handled by pretending indifference towards what has aroused our consciousnesses. Sitting at the table and asking *what have these thoughtless objects have done to make you angry?* Performing all manner of unexpected actions opens a door to opportunities we seek.

I cite the corresponding quotation. *The concept we hold of the universe does not of necessity match what you think of as the devil. Rather, it includes it as one of its dynamic aspects.* With that in mind, we began to notice we exist inside fetus cadavers hanging on the walls. These fetuses hang in a section of the catacombs inside the citadel. This information had been hitherto unknown to our conscious awareness.

I saw not through one but two or three pairs of eyes at once. To maintain such shifting spotlights for input was not an easy thing to get accustomed to. Some physicists are now coming to accept the idea of the universe as a hologram. A hologram of the universe which may indeed work in an identical manner as our own bodies. At least, that is, in its essential aspects.

Our twisted minds together pulled free as much as they held on to each other. I wished to see realized and freed the transmogrification of the giant prisoners. She cared nothing for others. There is us, and there is the rest, she said. Nobody will come to save you, and nobody cares whether you perish, however you perish.

I was, as she was, but leaves on the cosmic tree. We squished ourselves between the lines of the learned elite. We had risen above select civilizations by sideways attainment. We applied an unspoken and forbidden method open to none. but arrived at through a skewing of norms.

We had broken the cosmic egg by our heretical tendency. Fusing in sexual ecstasy and driving our curious and ever-open eyes as flowers. The petals of energy tentacles lashed onto objects in the dark.

The ancient writings ancient religions are not theories presented in sterile report. They are at variance with the tenets of the religious adherents themselves. The original teachings are a stream of thought heretical onto the belief system.

The orgy was the concept recognized before our plastered eyes. Recognized as self-centered and selfish. Tendencies modified or controlled. Developed like throbbing blackbirds alighting on ivy. Everything under the light of a culture of science and devoid of a sense of right and wrong.

Everywhere, the system tries very hard to polish off an ancient dark. Its elements do their very best to respond and act in line with the code. Malformed male bodies with salacious expressions, thick lips, and black visors. Bad times are responsible for modifying and adapting our behavior.

Their uncontrolled ways, our clone reflections. As far as we can understand them, we hold them within us. This is our home, and in it we learn and practice proper or conventional behavior. From it, we know we will see the sunshine aligned with the frequency of the set pattern.

Were it not for this cultural milieu, we would be to a large extent ignorant of the spider in the dust. The giant spider lodged high up in the vaulted ceiling where the werewolf wasted away. Genetic memories of man, of wolf, of alien creatures, alien creatures too distant from us for empathy, yet too close for comfort.

We had all thought it part of the mind of the perturbed architects, projected into stone. Strange creatures which had been set in stone, we assumed, from dream frequencies. The spider in question had moved a leg. A being coming out from intermediary dimensions and onto ours.

The occurrence before us was no mere defilement. By manipulating facts, we pivot at the foot of the beds in synchronistic parasitism. And, thereby, we are able to convince all that secrets are out. We drive the point that further resistance has strayed outside the realm of the useful. That everything is pointless.

All techniques from our garden work towards a quick reaction.

They must disappear before they appear necessary. Before the subject learns the true limits of what we trample. It must happen harder and faster than he can to think. To take away knowledge through the incoherence and insanity induced by the operations.

To them below, the defilement degrading their bodies is a feast of sensations. To those like us, entrapped as watchers, it is either a learning process or an enslaving one. Exposed to temptation, there is no responding. To overcome the current state, we said to each other, we must settle into complacency, and so we did.

Those around us who squirmed weaved the trap for themselves. It was a sort of mental activity that led them to occupy their places in the greater maze. At the same time, my delicate ghost continued to perform its various roles.

The impulse to become deceptive, to hide fatigue, results in the brightness. A splendor of terror shines through the technological woodland. The world turns unreal as patience runs out. All freshness squeezed out, we do not insist any longer on living a different life.

The closest way I can explain what this place was is by asking you to remember purgatory. But your memory might fail you, or it might be dependent on a different myth from the one I remember. There was nothing vague about this. There was nothing otherworldly about it either.

I had been transported elsewhere. And the link to that other being, the female, consisted in a cruel, bodiless vice. Slaves to each other, unwanted and unwilling. We had come together in lustful hatred and were not inextricably joined by an ethereal debt.

Vacuity exploited, the birds fly away, and discursive thinking leads nowhere. We were witnesses escorted away from the energy of subjective representations. Sparkling smoke, outer space, we carry it all away with us. Not allowed to speak to each other, burning today, whatever it was, and sleep settles in.

Dreams of further trespassing bodies that were not supposed to be our own.

We question not our sanity but rather begin to question what was first taught to us. The prison into which we were born, what was it? Who did it? A sense of affront comes from learning that the so-called prison itself was never locked. That we could have walked outside at any time. If only we had dared to dream. If only we had shut off the noise, allowed the incoherent crowd to pass us by. If only, if only.

Subjects recently arrived at the artificial facility will experience a manner of guilt. Here, all is sterile fabrication, nothing grows of its own accord. Serpents have mutated and abandoned the plane of the physical. Now only the deadest matter remains. Not undead, but inert, lacking a will altogether.

I still remember how we operated at a midway point between humanity and machine. Now, my conscience has absorbed into the matrix of circuits and synthetic bodies. I am uncovering new ways of being, uncovering new ways of seeing. Ways of seeing that were not exactly familiar, but tangential to my inner processes. Calluses of the mind twisted and ripped apart, the flesh alive writhing within.

Just enough pain to remind you what you are made of.

Nothing better than to take your mind off things. Only guilt remains. The guilt of sadism, the guilt of disappointing a god, though which god? The all, the absolute, yourself, others. Sensations spiral. Pathways that you can recognize, track, and decipher by paying more attention.

The flow speeds up and the subject's anxiety accentuates. His urge to cooperate, the only means to escape left at his disposal.

I have loved every inch of her being; her physical being at least. Once disembodied, I realize how much of a creature of prey she *truly* is. Her viscous soul passes through, presses on, its surroundings, and I can feel her smile.

I have taken the body of a serpent myself. Blind mouth on one side, and my tail ending in a penetrating reproductive organ. All bodies into which we can reincarnate have are the product of manufacturing. The descendants of humans being the culprits of this travesty. They have evolved and deal with the remnants of the old ways of being as they in turn dealt with lesser animals.

Lesser, different, opposed. It makes no difference. There is one will and there is another, and they are pitted against each other.

The moon of empathy waxes at the point where the greatest cruelty takes place. Pushed to the hilt. Not when an authority persecutes the slightest sign of violence. Not when existence within transforms into a vast ocean of still waters.

She and I have become one. Her presence swirls above my head. I cannot control her, this beauty turned parasite. Death has revealed who was the more conscious being, and who the lich. She goes on after disembodiment as a matter of course. I fed the insatiable hunger that defined her whole existence. Sucked out purpose. She swallowed, engulfed, and kept taking more. She made her body into an object of destruction and worship.

I kneeled before that altar more than once in a while. Enough to feel the cutting, the evil of her soul, and the way it made my flesh vibrate. Because I, too, was her.

Somehow, moments of lucidity drove a potency up my spinal cord. It happened with enough intensity to redefine a course of perdition I thought was set in stone. Try to think about it, you might not even be able to picture it, to savor the pleasure yourself.

Somehow, you should manage. And the more effort you put into creating that scene for yourself, the more crushing it feels. Definitive and alive, it takes hold of your mind. The ability to avert or escape my invitation, to change direction, remains out of reach.

We advance. Myself within this august creation of darkness. And she, worming and squirming somewhere in the circuitry. The citadel, a fortress of old, falls under tremendous organization. Its vastness and dereliction turn it into a cabalistic analogy forged into architecture. It is a dead structure throbbing with electric currents, electromagnetic fields, and forces beyond comprehension.

While still in human form, I discovered the way to traverse it with efficiency. Doing so depended on elaborating its form and contents in one's own mind. Its mapping for us had only been partial, given the fact that we only utilized a portion of the citadel. The governess left precise knowledge of the rest shrouded in mystery. The purposes of such a ruse, only a mind such as her own could fathom.

The number of variations open to the mind depends on experience and imagination. The more one has of both, the more paths open through the wilderness. I crawled through vents past the limits once known to me. The advantages of a new body are more adapted to the ruination I traverse. A transmogrified beast with the capacity for calculation acquired as a human. A vision starts to form in my mind's eye, a not a blessing in disguise but a paradise regained.

One must be careful, nonetheless.

The ability to lie increases with the selectivity of a certain personality group. Into this group the higher-ups tend to converge up the posthuman hierarchy. Mastering the skill of rapid exploitation at the moment of shock. after an artificial intelligence has taken a hold of everything and everyone.

Only by becoming more predatory and, at the same time, fuller of empathy, than both the most synthetic and organic beings, can one come out at anything resembling a promontory. A place that describes an instantaneous scenery, below the cosmos itself, but pervading it all. A non-dimension imparted by the creating consciousness, meaning us, in a state of perpetual change, in which the related concepts corresponding to before and after are nothing but elements in the individual's witchery.

The initial advantage lies herein, always with the questioner. From the outset, one must know a great deal more about what's in front of oneself than is told to anyone around. The ability to manipulate situations depends on the keeping of this secret.

For to know is not enough. Neither is to simply be willing and strong enough to carry out action. One must be silent. Failure to do so invariably leads to unpleasant situations, to disruptions of time, space and sensory perception.

The only thing others can and will be inevitably aware of is that the questioner somehow controls their ultimate disposition. Even if they cannot admit it. Even if they bow to you submerged in the pleasure that comes from their supine position.

People who in early childhood receive certain strictures retreat into a home of their own making. Dead leaves on the one side, and on the other to a very rigid and intolerant environment. Punishment for any display of emotional dependence turns into their living crown. Won't that be better than death?

The method consists of neither giving them affection nor allowing them to escape into an intellectual world. We are so transformed that our bodies turn into humanoid predators. Beasts who only crave. While our unconscious minds develop an extreme and sensual femininity. A femininity that detaches itself to the point of having its own ethereal body.

But you must crave it beyond all else. You must beg life to make you into one of them. To turn reality around you into a kingdom, though not the one you pined for in dreams.

The governess picks us, questioners, for the pattern of our minds. A pattern common in a culture where ruggedness and individuality remain the only promise of letting go of fantasies of a delusional past.

You are taking right up a staircase to high hell the shadiest paths. They tell us we will never again have to go through the trauma. Those of us who at a young age can put on a cold expression and say yes, though trembling inside, are at a premium for the bio-mechanical caste. The isolated communities are readiest. Their most tender hubs with which they can interface made available to authority.

The last thing they would ask us is, do you want to see mommy? It is possible that it might trigger the phenomenon of running amok. A wild attempt to readjust. No. They want every bone in our body, each leaf and bramble, every living unit that makes up our being, to vibrate at their behest and to the right signals.

Bred for this work, the questioner confronts the subject with a sense of sexual pleasure. Physical stimulation trained into them but never manifested. Manifestation, you see, would break the power arising from the delicate tension.

He presents a dossier and explains that he has complete knowledge of the prisoner's mind. And who is this prisoner? It depends on the situation. They may be the rebellious remnants of the past society. A society collapsed inwards, and clinging to a rural fantasy. Sometimes they are candidates grown too old and rigid for inception into the program.

Every significant happening in their lives can is available. Rummaged, select information may serve the kinds of states and trances preferred. The sequence is not random, neither is it purposeless. The questioner as a child accepted, a child that showed the right inclination, is first left alone.

Boredom, or what to others may manifest as negative, further tests the child. It all comes down to this. Will he manage to have fun, to summon memories of warmth out of thin air? Development will depend on how he responds to false olive branches extended to him. It will also depend on the capacity to self-regenerate.

Social withdrawal symptoms are later tested for and taken note of. Rejection and defensiveness do not mean the same in every case. Hurt and misery can either destroy or recreate. Insulation may come with a lack of awareness, but it can become an asset.

Directed hate too. To hate the very thought of certain unwanted ends. To see them as stupid.

I grew up pent up between metallic walls. Behind them dense circuitry relayed vast amounts of information to a central server. My shorn head at seven years old created a visible reality around me. I was later to lose this certainty of it all, being an emanation of a child's omnipotent and omniscient divinity. That double life, those two horsemen riding together, would later confuse beyond tolerance.

The absolute at rest with infinity would become a myth. A concept straight out of superstition. Its description of energy, lost to intellectuality. But as a child, my self-consciousness had been total. Running my hands along cold surfaces. Walking barefoot on the sterilized floor, never a loose metallic plate. I knew the hologram to be a mirror.

As I grew up, the combat lessons with the other sex became all too much to bear. I lost myself in the garden of delights. Willing, tasting every delicious morsel. Accepting the turbulence that comes with entering time and space. Struggle removed me from my place of privilege.

I now understand I was fulfilling an act of radical deconstruction. A dark night of the soul. I had to see it through and incarnate in human form. I knew I possessed a special destiny. One that would lead me to project beyond this human form.

Absent from such an upbringing is the padding of a normal human upbringing. Disciplinarians ordered us to direct absolute criticism towards the causal universe. They taught us to observe obscure intricacies in paper. We exercised our abilities to build illusions into our nervous systems. We praised the columns of data chosen for an end and later destruction.

What else was solid matter itself for, this preternatural input? Was it for anything but to create worlds of our own design, to traverse experiences and engorge our being?

Anything that serves a function deserves consideration. But its possession carries with it the condition that it must yield to us. Obedience is crucial. One must conquer and possess that territory without question.

Those with a strong need to please others will find themselves losing their own sense of self. They will find themselves disappearing and becoming part of a greater whole.

Relationships must be thus threatened every once in a while. We must challenge them lest dependence or acceptance falls into the category of a given.

Bewilderment and a fine amount of rejection are the preconditions for a clear sky. The world within the consciousness of the evolving being all that matters.

To sustain such states transforms the child. They must train to withstand their onslaught. They must learn to examine their cobweb intricacies, bright and ordinary. They must attend to the morning and evening stars. They must walk through that threshold of terror into future worlds.

We inhabit mysterious dimensions that lie between time-space and what lies beyond. Rather than inside it, through it. What lies beyond are the further reaches of the cosmos. They are the shores of dead stars whence living nightmares arise.

Here are horrors made flesh and given sundry forms and shapes. Hissing and speaking in tongues foreign, they threaten your normal consciousness. These sleeping lulls carry you from one place of your mind to its deeper recesses. They communicate ways of being that exert a bending force upon your exposed soul. Twisted positions allow you to perceive the myriad forms that reality assumes. Such was the world we encountered when we rose above the high ceilings of the underground city.

Outside, there is always a storm, thunder, and dark skies. The earth heaved full of holes, giant pits, and scars full of memory. I looked at what I was, a reptilian of immature emotionality. My newfound form could do nothing else but remember early sexual experiences. Juxtaposed images and sensations assailed my inner eye. Awareness of greater dangers shook me out in a fit of laughter. We are hurled into these worlds of danger. Thrown with violent force to awaken and develop the capacity for versatility.

Expectations are high. Failure means death.

I remained unconvinced of whether my unfolding destiny had been foreseen. I suspected I had gone beyond expectations. I assumed an implied distance, a uniform introspective role.

A giant worm with a ring of inward-facing teeth thundered down the side of the mountain. Sliding over the rocky landscape, it devoured all in its path. It did not belong here. An evil countenance gestured, and power made sure the monster arrived.

My body quaked and I saw how the causal relationship between events began to break down. The movements in the unfolding scene and the world around me became jerky rather than smooth. Their pacing was asynchronous. It was as if the consciousnesses responsible for each of them had ceased cooperating. They were now refusing to cooperate.

One could traverse space, could in any direction without depending on synchronization. One could forego the referencing of a common clock. Connections effected through random fluctuations, evidentiary of the primacy of consciousness.

There is a primary difference between the monster that I was and the other. The monster that shook the earth was more self-centered than I could ever hope to be. This is how and why it ruled the landscape. My contemplating it went on as if for days. Digging and prodding the matrix woven before my eyes.

The ongoing process of my sublimation felt more like friction. Not deep enough, but rather yanked out. Descending into the primitive heralded the birth of my on-coming freedom. It was the suggestion of capitalizing on my explosiveness. To use my personalized emotionality at will rather than as a reaction.

Dirty grappling claws burst out of my once serpentine husk. I rammed a rock hard and moved out of the way. The elongated monster pushed and crushed everything in its path. Before this god, the land expanded and reconfigured.

Her voice had gone silent in.

I moved under her sensual influence and cruel tutelage. The stretched meat of my muscles obeyed every caress. Yes, I carried out my duties and remained loyal to the hierarchy. But at a more personal level, at a more embarrassing level, I became aware of my dependency on her. She, in her arrogance, thought this was a one-way deal. And in her lack of awareness, lost ground in the battle for consciousness, and so became absorbed.

The rare cluster that we formed moved inside concepts. It applied to a uniform and proportional relationship among members of our kind. We created a delineated space. We infused it with energy, irrespective of whether it moved as a particle or wave. Our intent gave rise to a time of our own. A time that assumed a specific velocity anywhere we wished. A neat and predictable operation.

And then she spoke, her voice reverberating inside the walls of my skull. What happens when it rains? What happens then, in this barren and lifeless land of cruelty?

Of a predatory existence predicated on acts inducing pallor and dread we knew it all. Aggression is apt to be excessive and was inappropriate in other settings. But here, it was everything.

Here, there was no room for melancholy. No room to contemplate whether you liked the way the wind felt on your old leather skin. Having assumed this hideous form, you must take it all in.

My transformation had been akin to changing a machine. I had to become familiar with it without my prior consent. The key lay in assuming behaviors that broke my pattern.

Trust in the gods and goddesses above had been but a fogging of the mind. The only angel to whom I prayed, the eye under whose gaze I quivered, had been that of the governess. Yet I had never met her.

I had been jealous of lieutenants and messengers that came with a word of hers. They seemed to threaten my security. Before anyone knew anything, I started to slip. I squished the life out of one of them, destroyed the evidence, and lumbered forward.

I was the beggar that beat up the man who refused to give me what I asked for yet did not deserve. The droplets of blood were never wiped from my hands or memory. All these missteps constituted lessons in my now spreading and spilling existence. All these unfamiliar body parts, sculptures, racing to safety in the midst of a nearby crag.

Trembling with the passing of the worm, I never saw the monster again. I thought of the experimental captives, how I had forsaken them, how the feminine in me reacted, my engulfed anima, my sole prime mover.

The purpose it served in my life was simple. A reminder of the precariousness of my condition. And yet, a different thought, not mine, to be sure, made its way through the synapses of the thing I had become.

The female in me understood and made it known to me. Loud and clear. The titan we had encountered was something we must aspire to. Here was the possibility of wreaking havoc beyond our wildest dreams. It could be grasped by going through as yet unimaginable ordeals.

How she purported to possess knowledge of this kind, she cared not to explain. Nor was its truth particularly important to me. The changes that such an intent effected in our biochemistry then and there were sufficient to forge ahead, come what may.

Animalistic, conservative, and lacking versatility. No one cares. Other mortals will need to objectify things to relieve their own pangs of hatred. One may be cautious and lacking ambition due to comfort, but oppressive conditions launch the soul into apathy and despair. A situation so dire self-loathing will trigger extreme overcoming.

You may walk here when I've gone.

Self-sacrificing giver that you may be, you know nothing. Familiar situations produce nothing except more of the same. You have learned but that the death that draws itself longer and longer. It is the most beautiful of all deceptions. The fall of man into a consuming abyss.

Our art lies in stripping anyone of their humanity long before their body makes contact with the hard surface that shatters their bones and sends limb and viscera splattering in every direction.

The questioner who senses during the opening phase that you contemplate beauty even in something as death will readily assume he is hearing a cover story. What you believe to be your dearest convictions and memories, he discards as something that hardly matters. What matters is the leverage they give him over you.

Resist the natural impulse to demonstrate what shines forth from you. It is all false. It is better to leave an avenue to the abdication of what you thought was your humanity, your escape.

Herein lies the only means by which the subject can correct themselves, on a night that is not what they may think. The possibility lies within your grasp to reverse your story without looking foolish. Enter the fire. Embrace the sun-death.

Dream of a huge dragon. equal parts organic bone and muscle. Soul-containing machinery, electronic circuitry. Its tail curled, too large for the metallic halls where it came back to life. It has no eyes to see but rather senses the space around itself in an expanding sphere about it. Each hand has nine fingers.

What happens when you close your eyes and remember? There, behind that veil of darkness?

Curled under a rock, heaving breast, silent screams in the distance, the past assailed me. The need to be very loyal to those who gave me support drove me. There was no alternative.

Guidance and direction were my only point of personal contact. Nothing to soften the impact. No friends. My only god was a cold one. And I soon discovered that nourishing it with my breath gave me strength in return.

Distress produces an inner conflict. It is the slow death that comes from frequent negative experiences. Where needless light gets shown on every nook and cranny, every crevice of your being. Soon you become all too susceptible to seduction, followed by extreme guilt. Mockery is but a device in the service of discovery.

Pierce through the veneer. You will discover in each moment something more. More than the holographic influence you exert on your vicinity. You will encounter the energy patterns left by other things.

The secret is that every single thing lives under its structural constitution. And each remains invisible in the daylight, but very much so present, in an out-of-body state.

Thoughts themselves, a pattern. When treated with due respect and attention, they reveal. They are as tangible as anything else. The more aware you become, the more you give life. You blow the breath of life into everything you thought was intangible. This is the truth of the universe. Your knowledge of it is a setting of the stage. Your application of such knowledge, a new stage in evolution.

Desire moves the flesh.

It seemed as if I had crawled and hidden across leagues of ruin and desolation. Her voice, ever quiet, I suspected dead now that pleasure and comfort had all but vanished. Or was she this desire moving inside me, now fully my own and driving my every action toward survival?

I was suffering what we may call the highest kind of hypostasis. Unfolding with every possible option of my existence. Shaping the very foundation of everything real to me. That is to say, my immediate surroundings at each moment in the deception that is time. I entered that door to sensation within. My experience is one of total desperation and suffering.

The most sacred method of fruition is communion with our flesh.

Questioners may feed on the subject. They are cannibals in every sense of the word. The subjects who believe they can fool us are especially succulent. Their attempted smuggling of letters from zealots was all but impossible. The invisible hierarchy was a fiery eye that saw all and burned all.

Their vital fluids drain unbeknownst to their agitated consciousnesses. Operations courtesy of specialized technology. What selects them is their treachery. Their impulse to self-destroy.

Withdrawn information that is difficult to extract ruptures within a new home. Direct questioning and auto-projection, lead to a state of perpetual epiphany. Effervescence in an experiencing of the divine. It all leads to desiring a final unity with their captors. A dissolution of their will and total integration with the higher powers. The oldest trap for the weak of mind. Recycled slaves in a cosmos made by and for those who would rule themselves.

A glorious trap for the ages. A ruse for eternity.

I searched for an entrance. A way back into the labyrinthine underworld. The from which I found myself banished. Remembrance of their pain gave me strength.

Their psychological cluster tends to remain responsive. It depends upon the external environment that we provide. We could watch them die forever, in the deepening shade. To a degree, the questioners themselves could become fickle, involving, and perceptive. Few had dared to tear themselves apart, to let go of that final refuge.

The interests of the guild were primarily empirical rather than intellectual. There was a chance for us, if we asked, to have our souls exiled from what was ultimately pointless drudgery.

A mountain loomed ahead. I slid like oil from the lamp, forging ahead. I tried determining the cause of any resistance I might encounter. I moved beneath a moon unchanging across the seasons of our lives. Birds transformed themselves into gusts of wind. Dead on my tracks, I noticed a glow. Breathing, muttering, and a burning sensation. A sudden longing. Humanity restored in a way that no human voice can convey.

She stood, immaculate in her vertical chamber, white as bone and surrounded by esoteric machinery, eyes closed, she smiled, her mind far off. No two questions coming out of her mouth are ever the same. Her watery voice, shaping each sentence and phrase. A vain personality beyond all humanity.

Only after due protocol would she allow a strategy to develop. The strengths and weaknesses of visitors brought under thought control. Visitors before her throne room placed their sanity at her disposal. Only then would she step down from her artificial shell, this Venus incarnate.

Don't walk around, she warned one of her attendants. Fail to heed my words and all you'll be able to do is lay prostrate for the pleasure of others.

In the extreme, the nymphs that surrounded her were selected for their ambulatory and schizoid tendencies, with the sole requirement that they should be socialized.

Did you get up and start to walk around on purpose? She would ask to ascertain the degree to which their minds had started to give way to something altogether more alien.

These young specters were incapable of developing reciprocal involvements with anyone else but the governess. She would present them with a finger to lick with their eyes closed, waiting for more, sliding inside. Smoothly, though not without malice.

They were adjusted to drug addiction of all types and encouraged to develop fetishes of all descriptions, volatilizing their unique adjustment pattern, extending the guiding hand of violation and ruination over it.

Led over a long and perilously narrow bridge, the mental engineers expected some of the attendants to fall into the abyss on either side. Yet, they had been pre-selected, they had been given a manner of training. What would reveal their character, and what they could become, would be dictated by their own lack of perseverance. And in other cases, by a ritualization of ideas.

Without the ability to be devotedly present, all eyes and ears, psychosis would occur. The only testable path was through the valley of shadow and death.

The purple mystery, the long-range goal of training these elite individuals who would even at a young age lord over the questioners, was to obtain from human potential all that was useful, fold it onto itself, and extract even more. The industrialized methods of old had proven to be a complete failure, leading the organism to retrogress, degrade, and mutate into barely conscious scum. Instead, the gruesome path made only strategic use of cold violent abuse, and not on everyone. The delicate rapier worked far better than the sledgehammer when it came to fostering evolution.

The huge reptilian statue behind the governess' throne and sleeping chamber exhaled mist. It happened at times when the capacity for resistance was tested. Only those of the inner circles had knowledge of secret methods. Only they had access to the requisite mechanisms.

Cooperative attitudes aroused suspicion. Those who came only to serve were devoured, their carcasses thrown out the high window of the tower. Once you made it this far, all servile attitudes had to be discarded.

Respect was a whole different matter. Utter respect was expected and enforced. The difference could only be told by a subset of the human population. The rest were allowed to wallow in their insignificance. Crushed underfoot. Replaced. Over and over again.

How did I come across this knowledge, given my position, you say? That, I was allowed by virtue of special talents. My access was, for all intents and purposes, clandestine, to be sure. I had no qualms about trespassing, for I am the only god of my world.

Mine was a painful reluctance to give into the system, feeling its jabs and tugs. The primary difference between myself and the other questioners lay in the means of controlling my mental activity, my propensity for fantasy, and my autistic tendency.

I scraped the bloody walls raw of anything I could feed on, physical, mental, or psychical. I was ever-present. A little devil that through mental discipline and diversity fostered a spontaneity foreign to his makeup. For a long time, I thought of what I had become.

Securing favors from the engineering officers by catering to their egos and fetishes. Mental repression gives way to precise intellectual activity. An iron mind is born forged with the sole object of becoming more detached. And what you owe autistic withdrawal to you can imagine being predestined.

Nature does not appear amenable to creative pursuits, to what was of old labeled as natural. At the same time, the primitive layer of this closed imperium prays night after night. It is a religion designed and engineered by a bug in the governess' mind.

A less perceptive questioner would have objected that it did not seem to be working the way it was planned. But you would know the chaos had been factored into the equation. The words were allowed to echo, to create and destroy of their own accord. The masses would strive for spiritual perfection. They would think of themselves as a divine creation. Their potential for fantasy was exploited without mercy. Their range of responsiveness unfolded over a web of lies. Arachnid handlers spread deceit at will and for fell purposes.

Being let down and bitter, the primitives dreamed about peace. They knew only peace, in their heart of hearts. It was never created; it could never come to be. For then, what would all these people look forward to if not peace?

These are the reasons for the plan, a fluctuating disposition of variables, ever-changing variables within preconceived parameters which ensure total domination by those above. Hence, more energy is required to become the kind of ass with the grit to know when to obey and when to stand his ground.

The somersaults necessary to stand within reach of victory are inhuman. The courage necessary to grasp it all, more so. But the desire to devour it for your ends was all too human.

You condemn yourself. You disguise laziness through your reluctance to act, to detach yourself. *To reason.* Otherwise, the world would be yours, this very moment. And this is all barely even hard.

Allow experience to slide, to slither past the darkest moments of your life. Keeping your single eye open, attentive to all that may come your way. Then you will have stepped sideways, into yourself.

We are the people who seek to control, to contain. We are the light rising on the cold structures of our individuality. We harness our tendency toward the river of autism. The sun is the source whence we spring by becoming externally non-involving.

From the fields of the earth, we cultivate a non-emphatic social ability. Our minds bend, lay bare, and elate. We want nothing but to see the villages laid to waste from our castles. We want to see others struggle in their rise and fall headlong to their demise.

During our infancy, succor dependency rails against the injustice of life. I speak to you, under the inconsequential weight of your thoughts. To you at daybreak. Those within our convergent cluster who manage to foster independence. Those who also tend toward the authoritarian.

You do not wish to see them angry, angry at anyone once the murderous fire is kindled. How their demons project outward transforms their whole being into an armored ghost. In the solitude of their minds, they invoke the rage of gods and devils.

Never recant.

We are also the dead, the pale, and the ghastly. And we embrace our state of in-betweenness. On the training grounds, we are allowed to talk without interruption. Those that become shades reveal significant facts. They were but one more time-bound corpse overlooked. Persistent, but resistant to change.

I hope that does not offend you.

Those lacking appropriate interests integrate all that is personal towards an ultimate utility. To be so trapped could have happened to anyone. Anyone inclined to persevere despite setbacks or obvious incompetence.

Nothing anyone could have done would have helped you. No one would serve as a proxy to your sunrises. It would all have to be you. The act of profanity becomes a shaking energetic event. Here is the pulsing beat of damnation, the satanic cause of all action.

Within the cocoon of that first reverberance, the fetus of your pre-pubescent soul moves toward desire. An act of creation that triggers true existence.

The guardians drove us from our cybernetic prisons. Through dark wide corridors we ran, and into open clearings. The mechanical maze taught us irrevocable lessons.

Some of these lessons led the quavering quicker into death without qualms. To others, the required application and concentration lead to living longer. It sent them into an excruciating and torpid demise of the soul.

To be effective, a capacity for bone-chewing brutality must be brought forth.

One must learn to deny, avoid, and defend against the pain that mauls the flesh. The passing of time brings to light the distraction and inconsequential relations. The social component is but a distraction.

Hour after hour, day after day, month after month, we moved rocks, learned how to fight each other, how to *kill* each other. Little mutilations marked on our flesh were our prize and evidence for ascendancy up the ranks of accomplishment.

Everything is movement, everything in the tangible world, said our bio-mechanical masters. Learn that there are no objects. There is only concentrated thought. You shall become movement itself. Learn to grasp death in dreams and you shall learn to deliver its blessing in vigil. And so, we were built by day and night.

No adjacent moment was left unoccupied, nor allowed to become purposeless. Even daydreaming was weaponized. The cosmos shown to us was that of infinite battle. We drew a path in our minds of endless ascension towards stars yet undiscovered. Our minds wandered through galaxies that we would never finish conquering.

The fixity of an axis that all human beings seek is not that of an earth or a sun, but the spinal column. Around it, the natural frequency propels a perpetual becoming. It persists into the revelation of character through experience. Determinism and free will are both true. Only those who can make full use of the power of paradox may live in peace.

Directed to exaggerate the reality and involvement of the voices in our heads, a new insomnia is accused into us. It is a perpetration of the worst kind, instilling fear of being the tangibility of heavy matter. Upon hearing these remarks, a recording fires off in the chamber, triggering a contraction in the trainee. They may begin to confess to the truth of a time without, to a crime they have never committed, but a crime that someone else has in truth committed. The wracks of soul pain still move through him as a vessel of the lesser guilt.

Of time it is only known that bodily harm provides a way to move across it at will. Without attrition except that of the harmed body itself. It is as if pain provided an alibi accepted across dimensions.

This is how the divine becomes human. This is how the blood of the moon bleeds down to the bare ground. A making of forms never seen. A building of structures satiating the searing call of evil wills.

The corresponding assembly of convergent clusters so selected calls to mind the self-damnation of the rebel hosts in hell. The flesh of the child might ignore such a calling. No matter. The soul has magnetized itself through misdeeds and indulgences across cosmic cycles of reincarnation. Dark karma engorges such beings.

It is our own pulse that condemns us, distilled as it is from pure desire. Everything in us thus collapses without resistance. The violence we wield like a tornado around our lidless cyclops eye quells a mortal calm. And our whole being turns to contemplation. It is an endless sculpting of moments that break the fixity. A fixity endured by the wild, the crude, the crass, and the innocent.

The etheric keys to a sacred stillbirth, hailstones slashing from workings, gnostic turbulence. At the garden is a gate guarded by a cripple. What is it that he sings in his mechanized chair?

Beside him is a little girl who smiles at the crying wailing voices of others. A girl the cripple lifts with one hand, silent with her cryptic smile. Note how she turns eight times like a top spun by the hand of God.

And external to you, you've figured now is the right time to see if you can make your gentle approach. The specters are real, more real than flesh and blood fears, more beloved than the one who screams with you.

Intermediate dimensions limit more than they liberate. The physical state is paradise itself. This is lost within the minds of the sleeping sheeple who seek some far-off release. They ignore the rebel hosts of the giants of old who fought tooth and claw. Those who submitted their souls to eternal torture.

It is because of them that you can enjoy the pleasures of the flesh, the joys of pain, the tears of love. To them, you owe respect and allegiance. Never forget Herakles, the hero of old whence all true cults descend. He is the liberator and inspiration for the gods themselves.

Myriad distortions impose their energies on the oscillating motion that shapes our cosmos. They are not uniform. Incongruities they introduce shape reality in ways our neat assumptions cannot fathom.

Here is where the science of old fails. Where the scientists held, tooth and claw, to the map. Where they attempted to beat the territory to fit their expectations.

In the citadel, the governess, an inhuman ruler half machine half alien, showed us a different way. The way of simultaneity and parallelism. Beings opened to both the past and the future, constricted into a suppurating present. All currents tied in grasped in iron fists disciplined by blows.

Whose is that pure voice, that self-centered narcissistic being floating across the corridors at night? A little faceless pup she is, a deaf voice she intones, breathing stupidity into those seeking succor, too sensitive and auto sensual.

That sibilant song, do you hear the voice increase in volume?

Inventive patterns on the floor and walls, scratches imperceptible to the imbecile. Of her, we were forewarned. Knowledge, gnosis, and action forged into the steel of a heretical path. An anti-path, a stillness in total movement. Such a path liberates the individual. It is without any meaning except to yourself.

Beyond the gate, you step only after answering the questions. The guards at the gate decide whether your answers are adequate. Adequate are different answers to the same questions. Adequate are answers that could only come from yourself. These may have come through deep reflection or of a sudden. They may come as the striking as of lightning kindling the dry bushes of your disciplined mind. No overthinking, no superficiality suffices.

Dare you come before them unfit and unprepared? That little girl by the cripple would have your eyes and tongue on a plate. And you would never come of age. You would never leave the cold comfort of the claustrum you complain about. You entitled little prick.

The wind quickens where the tree sprung hundreds of years ago. The tree signifies our transhuman hierarchy. It is but a reflection of the structuring of our minds.

Cell after cell opened and closed through ritualistic protocol, ordeals of traumatic clarity, of effortless separation of what matters from what does not. Questioning is everything to the individual, an ongoing internal process that influences all events that come after.

Our every role under the governess is a reflection of an inner stage. Her dictate is that nothing shall be lived purely mentally. Those who over-imagine and do nothing shall slowly be drawn out. And in their separating reality from mere inner summoning, they condemn themselves. They offer up their bones upon the altar of our goddess.

We will avert failure with the continual application of precisely imparted, personalized techniques. Temporary failure only bolsters the questioner's confidence in their ability to resist. Their ability to stand up and try again. Undying and ever-present, the wave and the particle rule over wider vibrations. The knife that cuts dead meat. The knife that hunts as well. Those who offer themselves up all too readily for death.

It is wrong to try one technique after another in an endless carousel. Even if the ideal method has not yet been found, one must try until something has been extracted. You can learn something from any particular way of acting.

For what is being forged is not only the ideal fit. Nor is it the ideal technique, but the soul hardened, pressed into a diamond. A gem that shall never cease to be cut from the outside and regenerated from the inside out.

The method can and will eventually be discovered. Discovered perhaps by chance. But only after a methodical investigation is carried out. After exhaustion of each of the less suitable methods have been carried out.

The questioner tries to hone himself first and foremost. And his supervisors, the maenads and the nymphs know this. Their task is to be cruel and exacting no matter what the result. Their task is also to encourage attempts they know beforehand to be futile. For they, too, know the object is to build tenacity, to make the mind quick and malleable to an inner force.

Why transmute the human being through violence into bio-mechanical fusion?

Why chain the soul to a wall and beat humanity out of it?

We are in constant preparation for the coming apocalypse. It is the test for all living beings. It is the test of whether you have been attentive. Whether you have earned your right to live, and whether the gods should drown all of you once again.

Please remember to note down all the important details given to you here. Use them all as workings. Recognize the access to topsy-turvy worlds. Enjoy inverted moralities. Persevere to the top of your own pyramid upon heaps of cadavers, the only place to occupy. Hear that voice increase in volume, drink of that soma, heal, and come back to battle ecstatic.

At the time of insemination, use the technique to synchronize both hemispheres. Such a function brings about fruition. This is the process everyone completes to produce an out-of-body experience. The gate to this mode of being is REM sleep. Nothing short of willful relaxation can take one there. Nothing short of constant alertness and awareness even when sedated can pull one out.

Our superiors understood this. They had to drag us into this deepest level of ordinary sleep so that the spike in the graph could occur. The spike signaled the complete disengagement of the body's motor cortex and the springing out of consciousness. From the neck down only input was felt, but no control would be retained. To do so required a bilocation technique that only the most advanced to have. So ran the rumors.

Suppression of consciousness of one hemisphere or the other at will. The effect of our interactions on the next sphere. An inner turbulence. Fragmentation of the eye of consciousness.

In lessons before a tall, lean teacher, we learned to interpret these skills. She taught our lessons in terms of cause and effect. We learned when the appropriate space and time diagrams fit. We also learned not to adhere to only one map, but to switch until one that responded most usefully was found.

The protocol seeks to elaborate and project the creative aspect of our mind. The aspect that collaborates with the creation of the universe at any given moment. The holographic truth behind the veil of paradox.

A principal goal during the opening phase is to avoid all definitions of how we will jump out of our bodies. We are brought into a chamber where a delicious one lies legs spread open. We are told we must give birth to ourselves once more. To do so well, we must seduce ourselves into a state most conducive to the operation.

All our lessons had a strong and visceral component. It was sometimes enhanced by electronic and mechanical means. Our personalities would confirm themselves, revealed through ordeal. During the climb, you would be laid bare. Once you reached the top, there was a screening to gain a deeper understanding.

Unless time is crucial, a universal plan with no societal remedy is preferred. Totally centered on every one of us as separate individuals. We seek an ever-increasing understanding of the spiraling process.

Organizations that relish in squalor see the putrefying of the soul as natural. All group-oriented aims are derisive critiques of life itself. They all end right back where people become very active in oppressing others. They take anything that can set them free to hunt. Anything that can take them to the top of the food chain.

We were taught to exploit this lack of protection on all sides. For you. For each of us. All forms of intellectual discipline and experience thus gain an upper hand. The upper hand of an uncluttered mind. An unburdened mind. One free to desire and aspire. All in *her* service.

Make the children brought from abroad stop living.

Life is the search for the truth. And truth cannot be obtained by bullying someone into something they are not. It can only be obtained by rational, objective, and scientific study.

Feed them poison, the poison of god.

The pragmatist can only be influenced by his own needs. He is blind to the caveats of his ideas and beliefs. We circumvent this by driving the shards of our broken personalities into a conscious, constant struggle. Into passion aligned with essence.

We are made to choose between chaos and emptiness when we are first brought in. Taken, as all hand-picked children are, into the chamber of reunion. Chaos and emptiness, the prime conceptual forces of creation. We did not know the difference back then. Those who chose chaos were taken away, I do not know where. Those of us inclined toward emptiness were brought up as questioners.

The emptiness-inclined mind projects the cosmos.

The subject may get the idea that his relatives still live within him. They descend under duress or suffering. The hierarchy instigates such hallucinations in us. Our reactions are observed and recorded. We are driven close to madness. At the right suggestion, you are made to open your eyes at the proper time. Your cooperation or confession signal mildly to them. They are uninterested in protecting the innocent. All that matters is being effective, without fear.

Stunted humanity glorifies the selfless person. The person dedicated to helping others celebrates all that is human. Merely human. Mediocrity.

Those embodying this archetype are never to be found among our train. Not outright at least. Once you make early progress, you are taught martial discipline. You are taught the ability for cruelty. Sadism as an alternative state of mind. One into which you *choose* to move. At the same time, you cannot progress without developing empathy and restraint.

Let me convince you.

The fact is that those who avidly learn techniques reach a limit. A limit for observing and remembering. They see the expiration of pure grit. At that point, we must make use of a more soundless, a nameless approach, one that will work further on.

Thy darkened form, let it die by not touching it. Remember all the things that go around you. Slide out of your physical body through either end. Fight to learn well all the possible methods. Learn of collapsing and imploding so that insight and understanding develop thereof. The snapping of that astral sinew leads to the improvement of mankind in general.

The gateway class is a guarantor of ulterior capabilities. It grinds participants down to a handful of tumbled, recoiled souls. Rather guilty and disturbed souls, blinded by their tendency to remain self-centered. Their damnation and their salvation were the same thing. The source of their suffering and their redemption alike.

You learn to use most sleep for disengagement. The complete suppression of regular interactions. The effect of fragmentation. Direction and creation are confirmed and projected upon the screen of the mind. The religious subject sees you wherever you are. Mystical and philosophical groups take it upon themselves to figure out how. Let your passion be your guide here. Harness your urges, squeeze all you can from the sacred form you know inhabit. The sacred made most sacred through self-cruelty.

With enough practice, I learned to enhance other energy systems. My consciousness attached itself to a humanoid cyborg attached to the wall. The technique to break out, clicking out, is located much closer to other words.

From the time-space context, out will I come because less time per individual is wasted. It is an energy environment. One in which the individual's much-heightened point results in an out-of-body state. Its level of energy allows it to travel further. The state may be regarded as enhancing consciousness. The practitioner achieves and exploits with their full efforts. They come to realize what would formerly have appeared a futile promise.

Human consciousness can interface with the entire process. But it is also in large measure incumbent upon the level of proficiency of the individual.

The candidate will reach the point where he gains advantage due to his skill. At the same time, he will stand on a foundation to communicate with the higher-ups. Analogies decide the nature and orientation of these relations. They are interacting dimensions, intervening layers beyond time-space.

His frequency output greatly enhances and further modifies the oscillating pattern. This pattern defines his being. It promotes the drawing for potential. It accelerates the process of interfacing. Here, you have the choice of concentrating on the experience as it comes. We distinguish and warn against adopting a critical attitude. Observation reveals impressive success awaits those who practice the latter. Take these words and their ambivalence as you will.

Upset, my eyes opened. I projected beyond to the point of focus and a much-refined image entrained. What kind of creature did you fall into, the face behind the goggles asked. And I was offered the four absences, a secret of the trade. Time and the phallus for others who anchored their selves in pure sensation.

What kind of rat do you wish to become?

With his index finger, he pointed to those connected and impaled. Previous candidates, cadaver offerings to hungry gods laughing behind circuit boards. Once the disruption of their minds has been duly achieved, their resistance irreversibly impaired, they experience a sustained psychological shock. A hypostasis of the highest kind where their pleasure and their pain transmutes within their brain and sends waves of pure energy flying across ports designed to capture them.

The process may only last a moment for them. For me, a questioner captured and disembodied, the end game was uncertain. I had never seen these people. I could recognize certain protocols and code name stylings. They are a part of the hierarchy that I had exiled myself from. Ejected in heretical overstretching, exited during the false transmutation of my being. A false hope of discovering something higher and only being brought lower. Depression and disappointment breed the furthest agonies and exhaustion.

Somewhere along the way, I had failed. Or was this what success looked like for one following the path of total inversion? It was pure guesswork for most of us. Aside from lessons, missions, and results, all was silence. We knew we were more than cogs in a wheel. As part of this transcendental machinery, the cog had a different function. We were the iron thorns, the cruel extractors of pain. Bloodthirsty souls baring our fangs. Living out the role to squeeze something else out of us.

The polished black goggles on the face reflected my own. Do you hear? Nobody knows. Nobody cares that you are here. You should be content with the fact of death.

He kept saying things like this.

I simply was not sure what he was saying, exactly. As a questioner, I was familiar with the standard barrage of nonsense. The storytelling and suggestion combined make the listener far more likely to comply. Far more effective were these tactics than direct use of force.

They confused my memory. I was dragged through many corridors and lines of cells. I am not sure whether this happened in a dream. Or did it, indeed, occur in this limited physical and, I believe, feminine, body?

You do not take drugs anymore? The voice asked.

I felt as if I were walking in the desert of Satan. That forgotten archetype of ages past. The embodiment of everything carnal, every excess, artifice, and pleasure. All packaged into one giant fist of flesh and iron. When humanity was young, he was everything. Then, we grew out of it. Out of hate, thoughtless hate. Onward through Gothic landscapes and savage ruins that no civilization ever left. They were all the product of our collective imaginings. On and on my mind swirled, out of place, and out of time.

Move, he screamed, *move beyond this dimension!*

Part of his enhanced consciousness was inserted into my cranium with a needle. My eyes open, I could see the contraption extending from the wall. His cybernetic arm fused into it, his own eyes blank. Logically entrained in my frequency, exposed as it was, devouring. Therein a much more refined oscillating induced. I could not move, a tentative conclusion out of reach. Splinters and piss, an abortion in my arms. Thin blood in streams clogging up the suit and the tubes connected to this half-body I inhabited.

Here lies the sacred tome at the fringes of rationality. The beverage of the gods. Poison to everyone else. I drank of it, in my dreams. It was given to me by this hooded figure. I assumed he was the same goggled interlocutor from the world outside. Lucidity is one of my strengths. Out there and in here, there was no distinguishing between wake and vigil. I shook in my dream body, convulsing as the ethereal poison filled up the rivers in which I bathed and swam forever. The promise of much faster and more impressive vistas, a twitching of the soul.

All of a sudden, I awoke. I was back at the beginning. Back in the body in which I was born. Not in my cell but in a small room. Tall, so tall, yet so narrow. Barely enough for my body to extend completely. No furniture in here. Only the smooth metallic walls betrayed advanced circuitry. I stood up slowly, terrified and relieved. You would know this is possible only by living it in the flesh. A sigh escaped me. I checked the cybernetic modifications I remembered my body having were still there. This is what I once called home. What I shall always call home. This prison of the mind.

The ultimate goal is to put the body's muscle structure at the top of your priorities. You must eliminate the bifurcation echo. Let any of the hemispheres of the brain respond in self-contained rhythms. Rhythms that do not betray anything but your most authentic self.

Whatever side responds may be less important than the matter of focusing. To achieve an out-of-body state, that is. Meditate on the double nature of the eye. The eye is more constant than anything else. It feeds on the emptiness itself which abounds within everything.

That is the path that you must take. Aim to raise yourself above your surroundings. To those who have ears to hear, the information given here is abundantly clear. To those who must ask what else, there is nothing else.

I established rapport with my jailer.

His eyes, his hands, the way he used them, and the way he related not only to me but to the environment, gave me enough to work on. Enough to go by. He did not have to make an effort to fall into the trap set by my voice. The cadence of my words, whether written or spoken, wove a spell on him.

Either way, he would hear their echo in his mind, in whatever way pleased him the most. That was the point of rapport. The deeper intent, at least.

I determined to withhold my true intentions. to not let my all too harrowing experiences slip away from me, tell on me, more than I was willing to give away. I dissuaded myself from disillusionment, discouragement, and depression.

Sometimes you just have to do what you are told. The question is, told by whom? For it includes all mankind. The influence, the failures of people. The loss of energy disturbs states and tensions so common in patterns like mine. Ideas, a means of explaining life, all of them megalomaniacal. Mine no less than yours.

He, the one outside, was much more intensely threatened. He was also tempted, and so became negativistic about his whole role. Such a falling into desperation was not natural. Such rebelliousness against his orders was no accident. Little words, little encouragements. All proffered of course by my mouth. All planted in the fertile soil of his rather vacuous mind, the seed of rebellion.

He thought himself the author, the concocter of the nauseating poison now brewing within him. The causality of the cosmos, a situation characteristic of the inexperienced state that must set only as a second goal the rapport that may cause information leaks.

I bled this wound that so deliciously poured its elixir of abstractions upon my head. The structures materialized within me. Not the wherefores, as he was empty of any awareness of their plans and intentions. Such knowledge could only be squeezed out of their feeble necks through the strength of my iron grip.

Planned action, existent possibilities, information collection potential. Hard to tell. All sex is games. Though not leaning that way, I could tell he did. A young man fascinated by he who keeps him busy. To make him abhor his real masters, and worship, indeed, desire, his prisoner.

The extent to which such proclivity was to be nurtured and massaged, I had to keep under strict control. Too much, and the notion of murder and suicide could become possible. That would not do at all.

I was happy to be back in this body and would do all that was at my disposal in order to best preserve it. And to preserve its integrity, as it were.

The notion of hierarchy, the possession of a mystery never wholly revealed, had to be dangled before him, or rather, its dangling had to be implied, that his own imagination fill brushstrokes according to his own proclivity, desire, and penchant.

A state of complete stillness promoting the bifurcation echo sets my brain free. Free to respond as I will, across more realms than usually available. I require control. I require achieving a level high enough. Enough to allow residual memory to float into the waking state.

It requires sharp fangs.

The focus of such magnitude is to maintain the firmness of **matter** itself. Describing the induction of a subject, I established something beyond rapport. I told him what no man in his right mind would accept the situation. His sense of failure forced him to live up to expectations. And my drive to disable him drove him over the edge.

Fatiguing his mind through abstractions, paranoid delusions injected blossomed. Intensely intellectualizing, a murdering little thing he was, his life bleeding into pieces limited and abandoned.

He stood there, holding the nourishment assigned to me. Subject to my ministrations, leading him to provide freely what path was possible. Shapeless, the information seemed to attract practical applications. Little games to take up since I have nothing to lose.

In addition to the instructions, I use my total waking state. Changed, he is invited to inhabit this last reality I describe. Hissing and all. He has the right to make decisions, the right to do with his body what he wants. If he so chooses a certain experience to evolve, atavistic drive in an empirical-naturalistic nonexistence, no claim can be made to his soul by any would-be defenders of what is just and right.

What would you say of me? That I am a hypocrite, a wandering beggar, attracting attention with the cheer of a little kid? All I have is this skeletal misery, the state of deep rest that leaves suggestions at this point.

It is the natural happening of a movement. It rises in spirals by rending reality with serpent fangs. Penetrating forever. For as long as my consciousness lasts. My movement spears what remains of me. Steady and constant, I take what I need to survive.

I invite a certain experience to expand and evolve. It works through more entropic stimuli. I feel no need to explain its provenance, for it needs to exist but for me.

The only weakness to avert at all costs is the tendency towards idle thoughts. Let the mind wander and you invite death. A purposeless existence puts your conscience in conflict with the ensemble. You betray the congregation. and risks the shapelessness that lies without materiality. Applied attention, focus training. Practice the skill to keep it. Sustain life through any anchoring form, organic or synthetic.

So the old phrases from the prayer book possessed my mind.

Stop it.

Dream, sleep, wake.

The crossroads; revealed.

Those reasons and excuses, revealed. The ways in which we move disclose more than the words we utter. Unspoken transmissions of the multitude of beings comprising the lives we embodied, and paths gone untrod.

I saw these things in the lines on his face. A trapped, miserable being. His hair, long for a boy, was straight and shorn at the edge of his jawline. Short of stature, his dimensions allowed him to pass without arousing suspicion or drawing attention. Yet, he was competent and dexterous. A combination of qualities that made him the perfect messenger, servant, or eunuch.

Every time he brought me my food, he would finger a chain of little gray stones dangling from a string. They are not for divination use.

These are a through-and-through attempt to grasp the experience, the allegory. That hit me immediately.

I did not need to ask. I did not need to be told. What experience he was grasping was unknown to me. The allegory was, of course, the life he was living. The caricature, no, the parody, of his most exalted dreams. All the lives that had gone by, never lived. All those hours seemingly wasted, rotted away, spat on. Not by others, they need not concern you when it comes to these matters.

No. No matter how many times you point the finger at your detractors, those who have abused you, those who have failed to support or recognize you, or those who have indeed made their very best to bring you down, *the only one to blame is you*. You are in charge of your dreams. You are not innocent of anything. Innocence is but a cop-out.

On to the four quarters of the circle. The bowl and the knife.

Regardless of the differences, every situation distinguishes itself in the details. From moment to moment, it is you and the surrounding event. Immediate, always present.

I knew that somewhere in that small cranium decked with his clean lustrous hair this exercise was going on. He was too far gone and at the same time too attentive, to be anything but infinitely present. I got him talking about the chain. He said it was precious to him. That it had been given to him long before he arriving at the citadel.

To him, it was psychological satisfaction as a result of the impossibilities. I disclosed my own thinking, denuded of all pretension. For at the bottom of my heart, all I wanted was to find beings to empathize with. Others who would want nothing else but to awaken and discover their destiny.

His downcast eyes had all along signaled to me that he might be one of those. Those too disappointed with what the world had thrown at them to even look at things straight on. The mind split. Still, he survived by applying the smallest amount of skill required. He held on to the awareness of something. Somewhere beyond the cold walls bursting with electronic activity, someone remembered him.

Mental inferiority and natural disabilities. Manual manipulative tasks. To these he had been subjected, he told me, once he had arrived. Feelings of subjection had been programmed into him.

Pointless actions instructed, repeated ad nauseam.

He thought he might have gone mad were it not for the string with little dangling stones he kept with himself. He was very proud that even at such an early age he had managed to keep his sacred keepsake away from the prying eyes of the citadel's personnel.

I, an experienced questioner, knew better.

And I knew better also than to shatter this most precious illusion. Some lies do better to the heart than the useless truth. Especially in this case. The hope and strength of the lie could very well result in us attaining our freedom together.

The rite of congress requires considerable skill in social relationships. But she cannot see beyond. So he told me. Entranced, eyes glazed. She believes, and understands, even though she does not need to. I came to understand he was delivering a message. One not altogether willing nor conscious.

Rather than break the spell, I assented. Asking questions may have rendered the message delivered incomplete or misunderstood.

I stand under the light, arms beside me, my eyes facing my interlocutor. The point, I knew, was not to take the information. Dangers existed, to be sure, of it all being a tainted ruse, a poisoning of the well. All that was clear at this point was that the messenger was not in control. That, or he was a supreme actor. The physiological signs betrayed the former. A bet and a shot not quite in the dark.

For the most part, the members want to reproduce. They want to laugh. You could describe them as impulsive and fickle. Liminal states and astral projection lie beyond them. Unless, that is, forced upon them by the hand of an authority, benevolent or cruel. A hand that wishes to drag them down into the void.

Verbally-induced rapture and the superior hypostasis of the serpent's teeth. On the Western gate lie effigies of the gods of mud in groups of four. It was in his obligatory pilgrimage to the structure that his demeanor had changed. So revealed the voice now speaking to me from his contorted face.

His alien eyes bore the hallmark of an emptied husk. I have heard of such operations where the soul of the weaker being ends up in a cage. Such entrapment can be temporary or permanent. I could have considered him my budding ally. But my interest at present lay in the personality who referred to herself in the third person.

She appears to be more oriented toward males than females. Her gods make no attempt to catalog all the dynamics that play a part in her development. Initiation and discontinuity define thought and action, stopping the flow of emanation.

Thus she went on and on. Like a puzzle for me, the prisoner, to take and from it craft the key to my cell. How can I help in your development? how can I quench your thirst, and restart the flow into which we are all born but so few of us awake?

For the first time, she looked straight at me with his eyes. Her total presence gave way a second later to him. Facial musculature implemented in completely different arrangements. Dazed and confused. He pretended to go about his usual chores. He was too ashamed of his confusion to try and excuse or justify himself if he could help it.

Any event in the out-of-body state induces a profound quiet in physiology. Hemisphere wave patterns of the mind attain a further frequency range. What the utmost revelation of the body indicates in this context brings reality to a new halt.

This man who seemed to exist before me, to reside in the physical senses, was only an illusion. Someone who had ceased to live long ago and was going through the motions. I now knew why I detected a double living within him. He was both a drone and something else. I now knew it was a deity of some sort that had come to inhabit. Something slithering along the electronic walls of the vast citadel. A being whose phenotypic existence I had savored my way. All unbeknownst to the thralls who attended the corridors.

Whatever information had from this subject was only received in proper situations. Situations in which his mind was more absent than usual, a B-state, that a warning would ensue and she would come out. What is the ideal situation?

Twilight sunsets let in pinks and oranges diffused into the ethereal stage we played on. I ceased to suspect him of being an informant. I did not trust him. Neither did his apparent possession discarded the possibility of his treachery. The issue made no difference any longer. Just because you think in such base terms does not mean reality will be kinder to you. And so I chose a happier route, one that opened up more possibilities.

Intellectualizing these things does not work, she said to me, at length. This was a few days after her self-introduction. Entertainment provides the ideal situation, his mind will go blank. Hence have I made it into an obsession for him to fixate on this little string.

He now projects onto these little stones a story that never happened. He did not bring these from outside but I procured them for him. To have something to direct his scattered mind. To have him comply more easily within the god-forsaken inferno we are in and which so many choose to ignore.

I continued to listen not knowing what was in this for me. I had no choice whatsoever. I was in this tiny cell, having found no ports I could send my consciousness into. My newly attained gift was useless in my current conditions.

He has developed not only mental discipline but also learned to be evaluated and probed. He can now open and close himself at will. He knows to pay attention as from behind an opaque screen, only such an individual can ask the question.

What is the ideal condition?

Asking oneself when is the best time to snatch. And, then to act unreservedly, and until then, to remain poised and relaxed.

The glyph of the eye is everything. It is the unity of impermanence, the serpent's fangs upon the flesh, injecting poison. Use it to its full potential. And so I did. I explored my coexistence in every possible reality. Explored within the feminine mystery inside the little rat.

My tastes have not changed enough. My primitive orientation can only so engage with a woman. Or whatever appears in its totality like one.

I needed to see what was behind the rejection and hostility. I ached to see the countenance of the voice in the night. To delight in the cacophony, the eternity of her matter. I am older now and know what the options are. But one such as her, who is to tell how long this Medusa has been about.

A supposed vicious circle ensues in immortality according to the mental weaklings. There is the dual problem. That of having endless experiences and yet having to let everything go. Ultimately, it boils down to this.

A philosophical idealist would, at any rate, be a misfit among the wise. A sad mess of hot anger. Anger in the face of a true immortal. An immortal is one having survived jumping from port to port across many interfaces. Inhabiting anything and everything from cyborg's brain to distributed neural network.

The cluster to which deniers, decriers, and opposers belong is that of thralldom. Whether they will it or not, and whether we desire it or not, it is so. Such appears to be the only way for us to attain the blessings of godhood. All and much more did she spit from her venomous mouth.

I enjoyed every drop of it, as she would later enjoy every drop of mine. To grow up and die is for the flesh, negativism and defensiveness are for those who tread that route. The sharp and punishing route of self-immolation.

But for those of us who move beyond desperation and become staunch upon our path of enthronement, the requirements are knowledgeability about the requirements of realities social and cosmic.

I cannot assure you beyond a shadow of a doubt that I understood every single word she spoke. But if you had listened to it from my position, putting yourself in my boots, with the full attention of one who yearns for company and to return to the fields of the free, you would understand much more by connecting to her predicament from a place of emotions.

How else would you have proceeded?

Would you have carried out a detailed study of her mind's organization?

Of the areas in which she seemed to have operated?

Her recent movements?

Or would you not have believed anything?

Would you have thought this was all coming from the servant, a confused mind in the wrong body?

Yes, that has been the doom of many, yet he did not fit the pattern. And the voice knew things he should not have known given his station.

Generally speaking, he is independent, impatient, insensitive, and intolerant of versatility. Contrasting negatively with her positive attitude toward change. Under her, his countenance lightened. The effect of his solitary drinking habit attenuated, abided. A mother she was to him, taking care of a son too often sleepy and messy. But she also injected him with paranoid ideas of reference or influence. Inflected on his suspicious negativism with predatory occurrence.

These were her manipulative tactics. And he remained entirely unaware of her objective existence. The background biographic data he had shared with me I used to send subliminal messages. That is to say, I asked about things without him grasping what it was I was after.

She alerted me to the presence of more authorities than I knew of. A mad Templar, she said, haunted the passages in full cybernetic armor. Something so far-fetched I did not know what to think. Was she throwing in complete nonsense to throw me off, or was she mad herself?

The special intelligence department could come up with such an idea. A clandestine guardian too ridiculous and symbolic for our day and age for belief. No one would believe it to be real when reported.

What did not compute for me was why I had never heard of such a thing. She said it was because those who saw it did not live to see the light of another day. This was becoming too much for me. I eyed him, and her in him, with suspicion. How did she know about this, I thought but did not voice it.

I thought it best to move on. To bind me to a strict and efficient route of practical action. Precise knowledge of intentions and backgrounds was not the most crucial. I could have all of those and still be left to rot in this hole to the end of days in my prison of metal and flesh.

My training kicked into gear, applying a rehearsed bifurcation echo. Subsequent stimulation of the right hemisphere heightened alertness. The operation interfered with the frequency range of my regular thoughts and emotions. It was constricting the unnecessary. It allowed all but the most immediate, and so most relevant and truthful, to peter out of existence.

My art consists in cultivating the ability to manipulate in accordance with will, desire, and belief. I am not religious in the conventional sense. Such manufactured cults the governess has reserved for those who would be caught in the traps of their own faulty sense. Caught in the traps of their own weakness.

Those who awaken to the functional nature of the human brain and its dual nature learn sooner or later that belief is but another technology. Belief alters perception as well as physiology. It directs the biological machinery into which the cosmos has seen fit to inject consciousness.

I am assuming at this point that what we call inanimate objects have no conscience of their own. Something which not all thinkers across the history of humanity have agreed with. Something which we might sooner or later come up against. You may thereby succeed in destroying all of your previously held beliefs.

She was so cold, this demoness in possession of the dull young man. I wondered at times if hers was the consciousness of a rock. Or that of a serpent. And through it flashed the role-playing skill and interpersonal exploitation she demonstrated. Somehow, her eyes betrayed something more to me. An warrior, but much more seclusive and socially withdrawn than she was pretending to be. Seductive and interesting, she wove her web. I desired her and the truth and forgot which one I wished for more. I cared not any longer.

Even dreams postulated require facts. They are functions that operate within the universe. We see them described in the spaces above.

REM sleep seems like a later experience of consciousness. It cannot usually be perceived with both hemispheres. The task astounds one at the beginning. One has to settle into the idea that repetition makes it happen. That confidence in one's ability grows as experience grows. And so I tried to extend myself, to earn the companionship of my only visitor, who had grown silent and downcast.

He operates on a gnostic radical. His actions match the number of interactions rotated around an axis, and I was not referred to any longer. The inhabitant that had once taken possession of him did not come through for weeks. And he who had once extended his friendship to me remained distant.

Confusion riddled his exhausted brain drained of energies by a parasitic occupation. Planting an informant was a well-known trick. Though few could achieve what had gone on by the confines of my cell. Now and then.

When he started to speak again he spoke about changing society. The result now is that he is much less concerned with himself than with how things should be. Learning to adjust to his life, he talks of prophets, thinkers, professionals, and analysts. Justice is ever on his lips and he grows wearisome. Conventionality does not appeal to him any longer. And all I can do is listen. My training tells me to listen, to absorb. To bide my time.

If there is anything I have learned so far is that everything comes of its own accord. If one remains calm and alert, opportunities present themselves. The eye acts on matter through acts of obscenity. These cause turbulence. An absolute dimension opens, and a dissolving motion brings us closer to the source.

I was allowed to receive carefully selected letters from my former colleagues. The shows of false support meant nothing to someone like me who knew the tricks of the trade. If indeed the names on the paper referred to the people who had actually written the letters, they too were aware of what was going on.

No real communication could take place. Overt or otherwise. Those who would inspect the messages had a keener eye, and any sleight of hand detected would mean the loss of a very physical hand for the transgressor. The desired effect I had to fathom more fully, for they knew very well what my station had been and what it had entailed.

They knew perhaps even better than I did the extent of my own capacity. I had to be two or three steps ahead of this game. I had to assume they knew I would know the whole affair of the letters was a ruse. And yet, one cannot afford to fall into that panic-stricken state from which all dangers appear real. Paranoia starts to take an ever more clearer shape in the corner of one's room at night.

My only way out was the drone, the messenger, he who brought my sustenance day after day. Individualistic and likely autistic, I had not suspected the sudden rise of his sense of social responsibility.

Was it your choice? I thought while listening to him. Do you care about this? What part of you?

He can learn by rote the interpersonal skills that give the appearance of a degree of maturity. Deceptiveness marks him, but not overtly. At some point, we are all just doing what we do for fun. I do not believe any of you any more than I believe myself. We are all, to different extents, dependent on succor. Few can truly exist effectively outside of an environment capable of providing guidance and control. But you can never catch up from the inside. You must get out.

I wove a tale associating myself with his deep levels of sleep. The visitor entered an altered state of consciousness. It was a deep focus induced by the right words, calculated after many hours of listening to his patterns.

Those states and conditions are almost totally disengaged. They were achieved by guiding a conscious desire left by. And through him, I came to know our exact location.

I trained him to remember more things from an REM state induced by a visual or an auditory signal. An input whose coordinates disposed themselves to debilitate. and finally activate the wordless locks that bound my cell, I will never know.

But the voice is audible to those who can remain as they were. Freedom is at hand and easier to grasp than most would think. Love lost, and second chances, are all the same fire, revealed in brightness. Libido rises with psychic dynamism. It becomes perception permitting the flow of matter and energy between our two nodes.

The steps prior to the construction of the plan were not careful enough. The subject was not properly screened to determine where on the wheel of eight spokes he fell. That makes everything turn ugly now. Abstract. The same self-directed motivation that rarely, if ever, manifested in him became a self-fulfilling prophecy.

The drone did what his ideological programming told him. Having developed marked motor skills, he thrust a dagger at my side. Simply ugly. I caught his hand and the knife only graced the side of my torso. I could not dispose of him as I needed him as the link to the feminine presence that had come through using his body.

The knife, I took away, the face, I pushed down onto the cold metallic floor. At close proximity and under the lights, I noticed how blonde his hair was, and how unreal his pale blue eyes. Looking up, it seemed as if nothing would quell his hatred and rage. Being the manner of man willing to take personal risks for high stakes gets respect from me. Courage and the willingness to jump through, to refuse to be stopped, will always have my respect.

In another life, another world colonized far off by ships leaving the planet, we might have been friends. We may even have been family. Had shared those bonds of humanity. But at the present, no such circumstances presented themselves.

My instruction came through and I hauled him like a piece of junk under duress. I held him in a cruel lock that threatened to break his bones if he exerted himself too much in the wrong way. Your sacrifice has been for nothing, I said to him. I said nothing more.

His type can never be aware when they have lost all control. Engineers of the mind put him to the task. And I could not tell whether the presence that had spoken to me in ethereal tones, and which I had started to long for, was behind this too, or whether she could be my salvation.

I could run out of the cell then and there, and yet, I hesitated. Hesitated in the face of my current interaction and contact. The mysteries of congress, the enchantment of death-like sleep, the illuminating vision, and other procedures crossed my mind.

The form does not exist. I held the human ticking bomb down, my palm on his face against the floor, my knee against his back, his previous exposure to questioning and detention evident in a mixture of defiance beyond panic.

Only now did it dawn on me he was the weapon sent to kill me. Sent to interrogate, and then get rid of me. But all the subterfuge, all the dallying around, could only mean his was not a sanctioned mission. The deep level of systematic trauma he must have been through meant that without the key phrases and codes inserted deep inside him reprogramming was impractical in the current circumstances.

Do you ever feel bad about your behavior, I whispered to myself. I knew well how negativistic he would be towards those that are the most attractive.

I knew the stranglehold of the flesh that held him. I knew his reprobate tendencies, of which I had made full use in the course of our verbal exchanges. There is no one world.

Selectivity in hostile behavior carves the raw bloody stones bridges that interconnect them. Anything that happens to you is always your own fault. Blame your inability to be selective, and your poorly established involvement needs. I can guarantee the ability to choose defines all of your reality. It certainly defined his.

I was giving him more, more to choose from. But the choices I gave him could only ever benefit me. An impossible task for a brusque and impatient person. The keys to inducing successful change lie in compassion and psychological understanding. My violence was minimal, only cruel by design, but never out of bloodlust or wantonness.

As he started to lose feeling, his mind became insulated. For if you want to get to the true self in anyone, the way is through the flesh. The strength is in matter. Matter is absolute. Target the needs, and you will have what you wish.

Experiencing out-of-body states lies beyond question or contradiction. It is a matter of do or do not. For the many, the question that defines whether they will achieve it is another. What is your element?

Beyond the dim light of intellect, it is a particular tendency that will achieve it. Namely, People without excessive expenditure of energy. These tend to achieve it the most. They are also the most quiet about it.

The second group consists in the traumatized, the bifurcated mind and tongue.

You can try and control yourself. You can incite the visitations of the dead. And the state of variations, you can travel through it and not remember it while yet holding the key. The only sure way of getting through is by controlling the world outside your body. Every manual I have read on questioning presents the dark side of the matter.

Other spheres have as their greatest concern to date lies in inducing a distortion. To invite a creeping sensation of otherness.

What one can see behind this veil of misdirections is that according to a different, more arduous theory, setting a single point of symmetry involving persons invested in acquiring enough digits, more arms seeking tangible objects through the mind, while not reliable, displays a clearer reality that functions in tandem with the physical world.

The sigils, the symbols, the programming, and the dogmas, were all for slaves. They time bombs such as my unconscious little friend hauled over my shoulder.

Obscenity stimulates all that exists in power. The matter and the body experience and interact. Fires lit in my mind, a suspicion against a single informant.

The low entropy state characterizes the fullness of my attention. It is the beginning of my taking back the material world I once left. And this body is the vehicle for the energy I have gathered.

Under the trees in one of the many courtyards I lay his body. It was an image, an amulet, that had rendered him so. Thoughts dispelled by a possession I had kept secret years ago, always tucked amid the folds of my suit. Like one would a hidden microphone. Short-lived souls cannot understand why I went through the trouble, the risk, of hiding an illicit object. We are what we pass, suggesting that the talk and whispers at the other end of the room are meant for us and reach our ears.

No torture gets you to hear what you want. There is always that little voice. The fall of trickling water upon round pebbles. More than brute force it is the darkened chamber, the frankincense, jasmine, and rose floating in the air, and the terrifying symbol that reveals being.

All these make an impression without the twisting of the flesh. Put both together and you have a repressed ticking animal waiting to be unleashed or disarmed by the right triggers. An eccentric such as this rarely becomes a true schizophrenic.

Each one of them taken to that chamber is given a limited amount of time. They suffer hardships and delight in prolonged efforts to maintain their sanity. Benzedrine and hallucinogens expose their many possibilities. Their soul is laid bare in states of insomnia and restlessness.

At the end of the ordeal, too exhausted, dead in the face, headaches produced by inner tension lead them to bury everything under a rush of noise. Such a blanket of security remains their only comfort, a form of apathy and mental confusion that blocks them.

The effigy I carried I knew to come from one such laboratory. I was not supposed to know, you see, and I was never there. The etched carving fallen outside the edges of a perimeter fit right in the palm of my hand. It was easily tucked away.

My own little interest in authority at the time made it so that I was never searched, as I aroused no suspicion. Prestige positions too out in the open for my taste caused me discomfort. Like a physiological warning shot through my gut.

And so I never did compete for them. I could move living quarters without arousing questions. Nor was it required of me to change my habits. My thought patterns could stay the same after qualifying as a questioner.

I chose my specialties by first becoming adept at them. I allowed my intuition to guide me like a hungry hound, and then attacking as if my life depended on it. Without authoritative rank, I extended an invisible influence. I did so by the mere penchant I had for independence and absolutism. Nothing was out of reach, but most were not wanted. I walked the solitary wide tubular pathways of the citadel back then.

Long tunnels several meters tall and wide were never far from a light source. The light source could be natural or artificial. Yet, were always submerged in a quiet dimness. An effect induced through strictures of protocol. An effect enforced by dint of organizational fanaticism.

It seemed to me that from the bull's head pendant now in my possession a perpetual murmur came. A composed vocalization comes from its eyes. I would not incriminate myself. I knew too well the history of questioning. I knew it to be full of confessions to crimes committed and otherwise.

The backdrop of organizational brutality did not impede the transformation of my soul into kinder forms. The more irrelevant the pain induced appeared, the more significant the echoes. The stronger the reverberation of other existences. The transformation is illusory.

What really happens is that you start listening to yourself. The rumblings within your chest cavity, the vibration of your bones. Your hypertrophied senses turn into the gold on the altar of your focusing intensity.

Thus, generally rejecting the effectiveness of force you cancel your own holiness. You come to unify what was once separated. It was never an innocent operation. In the end, you want to preserve yourself.

Empathy and our interconnectedness only serve to enhance our individuality. Or so we chose. Those who chose otherwise end up sacrificing themselves for an illusory cause. These types have their uses too. If you catch them on time, give them a female dominator and send them on their way. Then they will do the bidding of the governess under the guise of saving others.

Resting under the trees, my companion started to awaken. He does not know what to protect against. Instead, rises and strikes the air, dumb. He tells me to stay away from him. I observe him, all the wonderful possibilities for termination open to me.

Committing himself to intensive physical pursuits would have made a world of difference. But he did not. He was defenseless, even more than he thought himself to be. What course of action will reduce his ability to resist?

Using the forbidden effigy I still carried with me could undercut all chances. we had sidestepped active areas into beautiful but less trodden passages. Most organizational elements had no capacity for appreciation for such geographic corners. We were going to a certain location still quite far off.

This game he was playing, affirming to deny, lacking all significance, was getting on my nerves. One must remember in times such as this that the architecture of the cosmos is upheld by your gaze. Remember that it is only its fixity that unveils the upward path.

I asked if he was hungry, and the battle was over. No torture is necessary to neutralize him who is a slave to his physical needs and desires. This one could never have been part of a terrorist group. Though he was, and so was I.

We had nothing. Despite my hunger, all I could think of was how to make use of him. The sound of boots striking the floor in rapid fashion reached my ears. I saw his eyes grow wide and his mouth move. Too late. His throat was slit before the vocal cords could act, only a gurgle escaping him. I front-kicked his still-standing body to get it out of the way and out of sight.

The main tunnel that opened onto the circular clearing.

If everything worked, the contingent would pass me by, giving me a few more hours, at most, to figure out what to do. At worst, I they would capture me along with hundreds of other terrorists. Arrested and tortured, my processing would remain indistinguishable from the suffering of civilians.

Our ruthless society would condone it all. The best you can ask is how long it would take for the dead to visit, for their voices to become all that I could perceive. And from that darkness a plethora of minutiae would fester. Possibilities would molder my next transformation.

There was another, more important, question. Was I to go through all that pain to gain an ascension and lose the physical? Or would I use every means possible to overcome my most difficult position.

All that remained for me to do was to walk up that path of burning skulls, a step at a time, like a cancerous growth that knot by knot conquers and mars the sanctity of a body abandoned. A body that has long forgotten who it serves.

The part encodes the whole. Dropped from a frozen hologram, the number of pieces can reconstruct the whole. No matter what you think has been lost, the holographic progression would have nonetheless been made.

To interact with energy, the subject should believe that he has been forsaken by his comrades. He must feel the allure onto the path where paradox rules all that exists. Have the objectives of the questioning been met?

I go through them again and again in relation to myself. Better I do it before they do, that I know what might come about. Thrown into a state of disarray, I fixate on not getting caught again. A drainage system of sorts, under the rock, so far outside the perimeter. I crawl to it and pull my late attendant in with me.

Comprehensive admissions by the subject, his assertion not verified. I detected deception but had no time to resume my questioning. Exploitation and disposal were the order of business. But I intended our links to go beyond the merely professional.

I have yet to hope for humanity, a part of me, at any rate. Hope that we may admit to the necessity of self-control and discipline. For our own sakes. The need for secrecy and focus over and above the many useless incursions people choose to defend and give meaning to despite all evidence showing all there can ever be is a progression of higher levels of awareness.

Is meaning is chosen after the fact?

It is projected onto hypotheticals?

What they wanted with me after all that had happened was beyond me. I had escaped the fold, I had transcended the boundaries of expectation that met the schemes. At least I thought so.

I ignored any knowledge held by higher echelons or secret divisions of operatives. There were circles within circles of plots directing my evolution. Evolution, even at the risk of my life. They operate from a perspective uncaring for safety. It is possible they had circumstantial evidence revealing the next stage was at hand.

Down into the square hole in the concrete, I fell, pulling along the blissful cadaver after me.

Sooner or later, they will come after me. After us.

The sort of person that hunts must be aggressive in his denial of anything. Only successful apprehension counts. Like bloodhounds they must assume themselves correct in their decisions.

The is the sort of person to succeed at such an endeavor would rather practice their skill at a musical instrument, work on assembling and disassembling a mechanical contraption, or read procedural manuals rather than ego-building.

In the field, only the stagnant stench of death would remain. The blind semi-human monsters with augmented senses would find their way here. At night, long after the armed contingent was gone.

Gone for their own sake, these instruments of death. These were artificial intelligences inserted into mechanical skeletons augmented with biological growths. They were as efficient as they were unpredictable.

Humanity found ways to enhance their biology with circuitry. And it discovered that providing biological parts to artificial intelligence hosts gave them access to fields of otherness not measurable by scientific means.

Focused on what is ahead, I must inspect the body. I must search his possessions for any clue of that voice that had once spoken through him. The link to the effigy I carried with me.

Somewhere down the steep path I was stumbling lay the key to my ascension. The forest behind me lay burned with irreparable ruin.

General productivity and effectiveness result from preoccupations. It is not only possible but expected of me to extract all that is useful from even my most esoteric interests.

Such was, indeed, the structure and aim of our training program for questioners. My crime was not finding out much about anything foreign to my occupation and lot. The context served only to see something of value in each tiny little death. Death feeding into the myth of hope. Hope that held together the fractured and desperate climbing up the vine. The dramatic flair, the light from the moon before it dawns. Such was the symbol I created for myself. I was without a plan, but improvised from a place of sincerity and care, for my soul, indeed for my body.

I felt confused and overwhelmed. Prior associations of angles, rational and intuitive meanderings, decided my progress.

We all participate in patrol duty for years before our division training is complete. Before we qualify for any division. Those who forever remain here do so out of choice for a simpler fate, or out of sheer incompetence. Thus hierarchy arises in any human endeavor. Thus it arises in any part of the cosmos, organic or inorganic.

Without the benefit of intelligence, without obtaining full details reported, I follow the path of energy produced by the stimulation of my eye, the turbulence coiling and biting inside. I must wait to be on the other side for action in the knowledge of whatever awaits us there.

I do not like what is on offer.

The primary problem for most is that they misinterpret the external environment. There is so little that is different from person to person, aside from the fake taboos and the lazy pretense. Only training can weed it out, or a natural predatory propensity.

In the extreme, psychotic paranoid delusions lead the subject to what others see as bizarre and unrealistic visions and conceptions. They are tadpoles thrashing around in dry land. But I know what I see. An altar and the implied evocations. A more perceptive individual will deem the undertaken path as impossible. They will fall into the trap of considering what lies before my eyes as unrealistic.

My own consciousness breaks in two before these relics of a mythic past. I once dreamt and wished to encounter this whole scenario. But now I inhabit it, and it poses a personal threat to me.

Questioners must be clinical. We operate with full knowledge of the holographic properties of the universe. We know of the morphic fields of influence. By performing surgical operations we avoid crazed and uncontrolled expectations or dreams. We are to report them. We are to direct them and bottle them. But I kept them to myself, even back then. I allowed them to grow in a corner of my mind. I shut them out from the rest behind a wall that only a green wooden door allowed me to access. A secret garden hammered away.

I am not alone. These procedures tend to be little influenced by training or upbringing. A cord links us all that come into awareness of each other. We hold on to it.

We learn to handle the pulses that come through the chains that bind us to each others' awareness by external guidance. Control teaches us rituals that we must use to determine the appropriateness of actions in any given situation. Even those with limited capacity for intellectual and emotional insight can assume a semblance of self-centeredness. Sometimes, it is the spirit of those of us who are self-seeking that places barriers before the development of self-discipline. And so we must burn copious amounts of mind stuff so that we may get used to pushing a more expansive and unruly personality through the narrower funnels of practical accomplishment.

There is nothing mysterious about the process.

I needed information from the two subjects that now turned their faces in my direction. They could have been prisoners of war. I suspected them to be defectors from within the organization. They could even be agents in disguise waiting for one such as me to fall through the net.

You would have to think the ideas would be that clear-cut. The fight, the awareness, shook through me. The older one of them noticed, smiled, and I knew he could see the bolts traversing the length of my sturdy fuselage.

I have come to consider the emotions involved and the chances that they would cut others. Now performing a banishing, I lit candles in my mind. The way I view my potential for surviving my situation liquefied.

The flowing shapes that represented the two individuals would assemble a step at a time. I started by editing their makeshift files inside my mind. The elder one was in control. Behind, a lascivious one, drooling out of thick lips set on a wide mouth and fleshy face. A twisted smile certified by glinting little eyes under evaporating eyebrows. Survival meant wanting their pain and desire alike to be in my hands.

I find that the environment and the inversion are opposed to the will. Replace it with intelligence and an appropriate activity level. Age and disposition come together like all the other pictures. Clear in their intent but less violent. Passion disturbs the harmony. Harmony that would otherwise force perpetual considerations and interpretations of the cruel.

You see, you can't imagine that someone could have adjusted like these two. Here, in the middle of this subterranean nowhere. But in context, close-up tendencies needed them to find such a place. They would force aggression and domination. They would have to acquire different interests in this world. They were not new. They lacked the safety and assurance of well-being provided by others.

One that is less accomplished, the salacious one. Middle and perhaps even low normal level of intelligence. It informs me of the more traditional accent crimes. Violent crimes by which they have come into possession of this space. Territorial primitivism.

You may be right, the old one says.

He becomes very possessive of the relationship. He has to live in this environment. But I have the impression that he was willing to give others the benefit of the doubt.

I wondered at that moment whether he belong to that Universal group. Whether he was the kind to never make a satisfactory adjustment. Those who make a shift towards the sadistic. Those who only express tendencies through the deeds of others. His companion would be such a vehicle. The enactor of his vicarious and forbidden pleasures.

But I am equally brutal and ruthless in maintaining my own awareness and suspicion. Not that I care if they notice, for in the state of mind in which I find myself very little else except survival matters.

I come to realize they have unrealistic attitudes and impossible goals. They show signs of possible psychological abnormalities. Even people in the upper normal level range can surprise you. They can bring forth different things during the opening face of an encounter. These two could not.

Is there an emotional reaction in either of them or on your part that they might be able to detect by its strength and which might lead to the start of your intended effects?

If so, evaluations should seek to acquire more recognition, prestige, and status than you probably deserve with the intent of gaining an upper hand. And it doesn't necessarily have to come from the present spirit. Once you name the ritual *athame* and focus on how one may be placed in the dominant position. That is to say, the one that I as a questioner was used to occupying in my professional capacity and in the dispensation of my official duties under the auspices of the governess.

I bide my time in answering him as the pebbles representing energy in motion float in a strange array in the space that separates Me from them. Their agitation brings to me echoes of the state of rest of the one and a fear of the other.

To activate the trigger mechanisms which would make one hostile towards myself as he has become hostile towards the system, one needs to know where the coherent light source passes like a laser beam through the interference pattern generated by our interactions.

The moving energy, aggressive and demanding shows me what his potential vulnerabilities are.

The devil is here and he is the author of all material emanation. This was my chosen way to direct a cryptic but meaningful message to the one whose death was the end of the not wanted.

His eyes widen, the message obviously canceling something within him, and the infinite options that I elaborate on within me remain in silence.

I watched the other. In his grudges he is prone to episodes of paranoid outbursts. Controversy is a fundamental part of the art of questioning. One must reveal telltale signs. They are the many parts of the world that one wishes to construct and project into the mind of a subject.

Something of advantage might result. Here, in the total isolation of his mind perceiving the meaning of a holograph. Energy passes and fulfills his expectations but also arouses the deepest curiosity. A curiosity that survives long after. Curiosity that becomes adjusted by himself after our session.

Come friend, he says to me, I feel much responsibility for others. And if I tell you what I think, take it only as an option, a name, something I give you with the intent of carrying through the abolition of the right you are now engaged in.

I remained focused, pondering to what extent he was aware of what was going on in my mind. I relaxed my body and stepped forward. The brute moved as well, and I could see the primary area of threat from him came in the form of sexual imbalances. Now and again one encounters subjects such as this. A combination of sensuous and twisted tendencies. They have never encountered anything resembling discipline or control.

I know he won't listen to me. I wonder what the old man has done to get the closeted pervert to unleash his dispositions under the direction of his will.

When it comes to questioning, it is agreed among professionals, that a threat should grant the subject time for compliance. But no such courtesy can find a place when the object is in fact to hurt, name, or kill the opposition.

I pondered whether it would be most effective to consider murder at a later time. Until I had gained entry to their little social group. It depended on the older man's rationalization for compliance. They were alert at the moment. I had some kind of upper hand as long as I did not show what I was and what I was not capable of.

He perceives considerable rejection from me, hostility. But on the surface there should be nothing but indifferent. I know that he can see more, as I would if I were in his position.

I know that we come from different times, he continues speaking. You do not trust your own taste and proclivity. You have come to a world where such things are possible and I know, I can sense, but you're hungry for it. You want the divine to manifest within you. You wish to make it accessible as a condition. You would like to propel a mechanical process but only actions of a certain kind can.

What he thought was that the best way to get into my head was not appealing to my compulsions. I felt a need for inclusion, to find a home. Nevertheless, his gambit had been a very good one.

I can tell that when he is reciprocated, he is likely to become jealous. He will become possessive of whatever involvement has fallen into his clap. I admit, that I am just like him.

Taking educated guesses. Making trained lightning-fast possibilities. Fruits upon a forking tree of classifications branded into my mind. Seared through grueling repetition and years of application.

The third reality is that despite all this I had never encountered an individual such as him. Certainly not in circumstances remotely similar to the one we found ourselves in now.

Suspicion, aggression, bitterness, but not cynicism. I exploited these in my belligerent and competitive soul. They were the proper ingredients that remove all limitations from my own adjustment.

A subject may be placed under the tension of fear. And, at the same time, also be given a discernible escape route so that he feels that he has a choice. I wondered whether that was the position in which they were cornering me into.

The first part of avoiding the current trend was to eradicate all fear from my system. Something accomplished through the total muscle relaxation. Techniques for such a process were second nature to me at this point. And so I did.

While I was doing so, the lecherous monster moved forward and made to grab at me. Fear reactivated shot through my body in the form of adrenaline. My hands went up to my face, and my palms struck two times upward against his nose. And the tip of my boot hit his lower legs.

I spoke in a louder voice, decided to go for the diplomatic route in spite of the circumstances. I remained focused. This should have been easy. The absence organizational control rendered me superior. No circumstances with these outsiders could have any other outcome.

I know you, I said to him. From my dreams, I know you. Won't you take me, won't you listen to what I have to say?

I made the only move I only had left. A few moments would pass before the other one would recover from the blows. Though in the heat of the moment, I delivered them with clinical precision.

The man seemed pleased. This is the kind that years for recognition. He craves for nothing more than to be in a position of respect. He would love for others to fawn over his accomplishments. He wishes for others to submit to hi words. To obey his whims. And that is good and normal. Except, he was dangerous. Dangerous because under the influence of his primitive adjustment.

My impression of these subjects confirms certain ideas I had about them.

An alphabet of desire makes itself available to me, headless. Conflict with the preliminary assessment. A degree of unwillingness to cooperate. These things tell me something.

If the differences are significant, they affect those particularly prone to respond. Friends raped and beaten black in the torture halls above. What plans did they have for these two? Not all things mean the same to all people.

The relative lack of attention that one receives blossoms into new ways of being that do not fit into the encyclopedias of the learned.

We come to know that another feature of our holographic reality is how efficient it is. Out of all the things that could be happening, only those observed happen. They do so according to an accumulation of information.

Causality itself is but a special case. Reality is more complex and diversified. It is a phenomenon of apparition and willingness into reality.

If you can be responsive enough to the needs and requirements of others, while maintaining your own will to power, something, a tiny space, opens up inside of you as a gateway to spaces that do not conform to normal conceptions of creation.

What is stored elsewhere in the universe is mere potential. You bring it all into actuality. The grin on the old man's face told me he did not conform to anyone's expectations. It was I who projected onto him the idea that he was old or that he was a man.

When I came close, I could not really tell what or who he was. All I found was a lump, the annulment of my mind. And the beastly human that I had hurt was no human at all, but a kind of ape. No aggression came from him. All of it had been a product of my wild imagination.

What I decided to do about it did not make me proud. It did not make me think of how far my training had brought me so far, nor of the spaces which my soul could someday reach. All I could think of was I could have done better.

I strangled him, fearful that he might give me away.

Fearful that he might stab me in the back, or drown me while I slept. He was too powerful and unpredictable to risk it. I behaved like the best and the worst of my trade. I knew nothing, and cared not to know anything more, but I did not leave loose ends.

What surprised me, upon inspection of the living quarters we had breached, which were not so far from the place where we met my erstwhile assailants, was that there was reading material all around.

The pages, however, were torn, and some were bitten into. The monster was in any case using books as a source of sustenance. He did not look like he was starving. Not his carcass, at any rate.

A confession lies at hand.

For all that has been hitherto written has been a ruse, a way for me to hide what is behind the curtain. The curtain of a life trapped. A life in search of truth, sticking to formulas. Only the last transformation, disembodiment, and defiance have managed to disclose something. To lay bare in ways nothing else could have.

The stages of the black path lead one to spiral upwards through a tertiary system. Four doors lead to a selfsame demise, but different afterlives. I have experienced one of them as I changed bodies. Even the apparent return to the body I remember finds it changed. The original organic material appears to have been repurposed for my return.

The basic disadvantage one has moving from trauma to trauma is the inability to perform intellectual tasks efficiently. One becomes dependent on firm, consistent, external guidance, control, and discipline.

I find that the fight must go on, that I must keep moving. But my own double nature, as observer and experiencer, seeds contradictions that have no resolution. I should say, however, that action is always the answer. Not because the conundrums arrived at in the mind are thereby resolved, but because the real world, the universe as a unitary being, exists in one total state at a time. You manage to make it change and the whole of it is in agreement. You as an individual may or may not perceive the cosmic state accurately, but actions that occur in it happen irrevocably and incontestably.

The moment control is all but lost is the moment when cuts, slices, and stabs supply the bulk of one's expression. The key areas of resistance fold under the weight of self-cruelty. I engage in such operations only as a last result. Only as a way to call on those voices that once terrorized me and brought down the whole of my existence to meager mental capabilities. The test was this, to survive the terror and cling to life out a love for living itself.

I continued to inspect the room, finding nothing of use except some old maps that I put away to later peruse. To keep moving, to keep fighting, and to want to survive more than anything else even if the face of total hopelessness is the mark of those of our kind. What kind? I do not know, but I recognize myself as such.

The effectiveness of most questioning techniques depends upon their unsettling effect. systems of control are erected to keep you on the wheel, pushing the lever, and exerting force.

My argument is not one of higher morality. I have no quarrel with those who would enslave humanity except for the fact I do not wish to be enslaved. I know this may seem awfully self-centered to most people. Those of you who declare not to be worried about themselves but about others.

I see my train of thought as seeking the minimalist route whereby I can attain a place of stability. For only from a place of power can one be responsive to the needs and requirements of others. Rather than understanding or empathy, what is needed is power. Power makes things happen in the real world. Understanding boggles the mind and empathy the feelings.

Instead, the simple understanding that my freedom promotes the freedom of others like me will spread a richer way of being like a contagion, replicating, and resonating across the morphic fields that dictate the shape of the cosmos.

Flowers, birds, fruit, you may gather them all and thereby experience the pulse of cosmic creation. They are the product of a need for expression. A book or a car are no different than a rock or a tree, an animal or a human. You may one day be any of those things. Out there in the chaos and vacuum that draws your energy coercively hither and thither.

I came to understand all of this once upon a lifetime. Once, in a different body. Faced, then, with nightmares in the flesh. I made my away through in an environment where the closest thing to myself I came across were the boulders in the middle of the desert. They could have spoken to me as they trembled with the ground tread by monsters consumed by the single thought of hunger, never to be appeased or satiated in this world or the next.

I estimated the further arrangements necessary for continued detention in this place. I had no liaison support nor a specific purpose to remain. I ran out carrying what I could in the utilitarian compartments of my suit, through tunnels long abandoned, but whose architecture reminded me of what was once called brutalism.

To a questioner, such forms of unyielding strength and formative inflexibility that hide levels upon levels of precognition regarding the human mind are a work of art unparalleled. They are the unison of human mechanisms with synthetic sorcery emblazoned on the artificial human landscape.

The spaces I walked through were a labyrinth of some kind. And not mere utilitarian construction, but designed to last and test. I recognized it as such even though you may say that a brutalist mind would never so debase themselves. Never descend to such artful purposes.

You are speaking of a reaction to a subject not permitted. Answering to a four-dimensional object depicted in two dimensions alone. The reason why these buildings are not comprehended by the masses is that, being made in order to exert control over them, their hidden purpose was to twist and bend spaces out of sight and taste for the commoner. As societal projects, they were deemed to have been failures, but as scientific experiments, they furnished us with plenty of data.

I put my hand on the ancient walls and let the sensation on my fingertips travel up my arm and neck to the top of my head. We were friends, this ancient evil and I.

Have your eyes, mouth, voice, gestures, and silence suggest chosen areas of sensitivity. Areas you would not have given up to anyone, with some exceptions, to be sure, saying to yourself, How dare they, these intruders.

You lie to yourself, as I would have were it not for my past, and you confuse the essence with the body, the soul with the tomb. What are your eyes for if not to see what you wish to see, your mouth to cause others to give up what you desire, but no, you won't come full circle until you understand the world is a house of mirrors, and the game played therein, one of costumes and masks.

Even for yourself, you must put on a show, especially for yourself. I lurked through underground tunnels with a smile, not a smug one, but the kind of person feeling safe at home, content that all would go on as it always had.

The universe is composed of interacting energy, a hologram of unbelievable complexity. The idea of a loose component, an independent entity, is unthinkable, an abomination. What happens to you, happens to the whole, and what happens to the whole opens up experiences for you to venture into, to further your cause.

I carried with me a haphazard folio lifted from the floor of the now abandoned room. It speaks of these things and more. It is a collection of pictures, though mostly words. Entire collections of passages taken, ripped from, existing documents, rearranged. The object so fascinated me by its at-once divergent logic. The brutality of the voices came through loud and clear.

It all indicates a system that elaborates, a method to stimulate and transmit change. Secrets dripped from the book. Mock heretical interpretations and suggestions of things known to me. They were taught to me across years of indoctrination and application.

I flipped page after page, obsessing, even as I do now, about the half-meaning, begging for completion, asking me to solve the puzzle, to piece together what would allow itself to be, once brought into the fold of a narrative imposed.

He actively moves to establish himself into positions of leadership. To move up the chain of command, enthroned at the top of a hill, impaling indiscriminately the opposition.

The idea put forth was an operation in code. The words were not what they seemed, or they would not make any sense. It was entirely possible, of course, that words were meant literally, at least for some, for those incapable of distinguishing the myth from reality, the allegorical lesson from the demonic insinuation.

Holding his position by force, fear, and domination. The right gestures, and the right use of communication, it all boils down to these things, to be able to convey that you will only tolerate the utmost respect toward yourself.

The way requires sacrifice, setting aside comfort, to bid farewell assurances. Hunger assails me, and I turn my mind to my current predicament. So many words, so many ideas, and I do not know if I can carry them out. All I can think of is the aching of my body, the emptiness in the pit of my stomach. I remember yet again that words are wind, that ideas are cheap, that what matters is living on.

You are compartmentalizing, willfully blocking out. Cutting away what does not fit. Inserting what does, inventing, lying to yourself. And so I did, knowing full well what I was doing.

I closed the book and carried it with me despite how much it weighed me down, resembling as it did a medieval-era handcrafted work of art, though much less artful, in appearance and care. It was an object of black magic, the priests would have thought, the work of the devil, the enemy and friend of the Church, fully acknowledged then, gone underground, hidden, removed, mocked, and worshiped without a name, or through many other names.

To that shadowy figure, we now aspired, without cynicism or overt religiosity. It was all one could do, to take a world destroyed and half abandoned, and grow as a human, or what remained in us of that race.

The effectiveness of a threat depends on the personality of the subject. I was nothing if not the greatest threat to this earth. Megalomania with a definite end, it was, and there was no other truth but my truth. Remember that. You have nothing else but whatever truth you choose to make the most out of a situation.

We came to grasp belief, the idea of truth, as a mind tool, a directive to substantiate as much control over the physical world as possible, not from the point of view of the group, but of the liberated individual.

The devil is traditionally associated with the eye. The eye that conjures up shapes. These shapes are illusory and distracting, and as compelling as anything else. The eye effects a very real change in the universe.

To follow the way of the devil and its truth would be to cease taking truth so seriously and delude ourselves over to the next stage. At each step of the way, with every new atmosphere, a new, more suitable set of delusions would be chosen.

The path I walk hinges upon the dissolution of one world and the creation of a new one, the change apparent only to me.

I am taken to an individual cell where the blindfold and handcuffs are removed. Fretting about the fact cannot help at all. Only acceptance of the new imprisonment. Their removal from my possession of the book is of little consequence. What I was to capture from its confusing pages takes only a view. The specific protocols remained obscured from me, the spirit of the artifact embedded itself in me. Heresy was committed the moment I set eyes upon it.

I did not end up here. I start here. The people who apprehended me did not speak a language nor bore insignia I recognized. They were rather gentle, expressing surprise, even confusion, at my sight, rather than the hatred and disgust I came to associate with my persecutors.

I sometimes wonder if what others feel, or what I think they do, is only a product of what I project onto them. It places an enormous and comforting responsibility on one's breast. Extreme solipsism has its upsides. All philosophies and theories perform optimally within circumscribed limits of efficacy.

Such faithful eyes as mine cannot help but grow weaker and weaker. An inert and vast landscape separated my mind from the strictures impressed upon my flesh by cold, cruel hands bearing cudgels. The mind bent, the soul twisted, the feast of the giants of old.

Given the choice, to eat or be eaten, morality loses its meaning, its purpose, the better life, the life of good, the good in living. I have been disrobed and as pressing as my circumstances undoubtedly are, I cannot stop myself from thinking, from pondering.

I have laid down, not exactly to die, but to conjure, to travel down the river of time to figure out how to jump between currents of causality. No need to jump, or bolt, just to gently wade, making your way imperceptibly from here to there, carving a unique sequence unforeseen by the dark sisters of fate. The will to open doors, to destroy the mechanism, the process I must start.

A man comes into my cell. He is accompanied by two guards. Their are clothes worn and old. Their weapons unknown to me. I never had anything to do with arsenals or firearms, aside from the standard issue revolver. Even the lowest messenger was required to wield this weapon with deadly force in the point shooting tradition.

The precariousness of my situation does not escape me. They will speak words I will not understand. They will be angered at their not receiving the answers they expect. From my perspective, and my odds of survival, the only thing that matters is how I will meet both challenges.

I lack the option of force applied from outside. Everything can be accomplished by psychological manipulation. Until resistance is sapped and the urge to yield is fortified, this must be my route to walk.

These seemed like amateurs. Apprehensive, if anything, eager. More eager than any prisoner in my position should ever be allowed to witness. In one swift stroke, they had reinforced my confidence. Their nonverbals gave me clues as to their actual emotional state. And all I gave in return was a wide-eyed, smiling expression. The best of it all is, I was sincere in both my sympathy and my intent to manipulate.

I trained in altered states of consciousness to allow energy to pass through. To traverse the various aspects of my being. To perceive its electrostatic field. To interact with the holographic images conveyed by the whole.

They spoke to me, these images, even as I understood I was speaking with myself. The trick being, to understand that the same happens when you speak to any flesh and blood person. You are always interacting with your interpretation. Your image of what the other person looks like, what they do, and what they say.

I find the extremist notion amusing. Pointless too. To assume that whatever you capture in your head is the only truth. And then to judge those you come across according to your sense of absolute authority. And yet it is common.

I do not advocate the contrary, total acceptance, as that would be madness. You must operate on the basis of your own fiction. But you best be aware that it is a fiction. At the end of the day, of the season, whereupon you would move on to a new one, fitting a new purpose, a new body of knowledge, and, above all, a burgeoning desire.

In this unity, intersection points occur that are amplified and multiplied infinitely. What their gestures tell me, how their voice sounds like, what mannerisms make up their communication interface, all of these and more, I register, sequence, factor into an equation.

One of the guards holds a grudge. Against whom, I ignore. He is intent on getting something from me, aggressively. But he is not in charge. The man with his hands on the steering wheel of this operation, for all it's worth, is a much kinder person. He is out of sorts in the scenario, and he flinches at my nudity. The guard at his left, more congruent with his leader than the other, switched his attention between us, wide-eyed and expectant.

The subject is provided with ill-fitting clothing to decrease comfort and fitness. It diminishes his disposition and ability to resist. Following this rule is standard procedure. To extend, as much as possible, the discomfort of initial shock. To render the prisoner inadequate.

The hot weather made it so that the clothing was, at once, suffocating and a relief from bodily moisture. The overalls fit clumsily. My feet remain unshod. But I have been disembodied, I have been trapped in more confusing states, and all I can think of is, what next?

I am always left a bit empty, as if nothing were enough. As if I was never rested enough. Something leaks from me. And even when this is not so, even when at peace, the hunger never ceases, the will to consume, people and things.

Their presence disturbed me. It shook me out of the now customary reveries. But they also gave me a focus point that made life simpler again. It made life graspable, flowing, inoffensive, even the ugly one, the one that wished to hurt me. With each visit he grew more agitated. He shouted more, showed more derision for the one in charge, and I was no closer to any image of what they searched after.

Some of our desires and interests are socially unacceptable. Being required to check or control them simply drives us into depression. Into anxiety and guilt without effective action. I can see this, clear as day, but the one tentatively, temporarily, in command, *cannot* command.

Unchecked this one will kill or maim those around him, friend or foe. For what he finds satisfying, society has set beyond the bounds of what is possible. Ignoring the fiction this is, ignoring that among them many monsters walk.

I smile and look kindly on them. On all except for the cruel one. For I know kindness is wasted on his kind. Controlled confrontation, making him feel observed, judged, and so on, can at least precipitate an action on his part that will reveal him to his comrades. The danger to me, as a prisoner, is patent. A risk I am willing to take.

Reconnaissance follows the opening phase. Their leader is a family man. He is out in the open for me to see, in the form of sundry memorabilia, insinuating at least three separate origins. He talks to me when he takes me out for a stroll, at which time I am also brought a portion of porridge.

After a few days, he has dropped his guard a great deal. He does see me as a threat. No threat he can recognize, no evil intent, and, the truth is that there isn't any. The truth to manipulating a situation is to genuinely go through the states you want to project.

The difficulty in doing so is that we are usually not in control of our states. We let ourselves fall into them. We let our lives be guided by emotions. Emotions could be a more useful bridge between ourselves and the world. Or, between ourselves and others.

The path of action reverses nature and obliterates all the others.

I repeatedly empty my cup, the mind ready to receive new input, to adapt and learn. Repeatedly rinsing the system means nothing. It never stays for too long.

What can you learn if you go on like this, you might say.

The answer is, plenty.

What you grasp you encode in your nervous system. It imprints itself not just on your brain but in pathways patterned down the axis pole of your body.

When you expose yourself to an environment, a system, a teacher, their teachings, and go through the process of problem-solving, or the application of concepts, certain things become one with the matrix of body, mind, and more, that is your current iteration.

When we learn, it is the mind, that is, the interface port, that must be cleaned. You lose nothing that wasn't meant to stay with you.

Most people underestimate their capacity to withstand pain. Brutality creates only resentment, hostility, and further defiance. Brutality embeds lessons in hatred engineers volatile individuals. They feel entitled by their suffering to cause more suffering. They chasse the shadows in their mind while running through everyone else.

Consciousness can break that cycle. Whether in humans or in other creatures. It gives us at least an indication that the universe is not only mechanical in nature. It tells us that there are hidden corridors inside the halls of reality carrying intent and at odds with common sense.

Once such things are understood, the flesh is more willing to cooperate. The burden of inflicted pain turns out to be one more event the interpretation of which is up to us to choose.

The immutability of the surroundings, the foreign faces, disdainful ignorance, it was all part of my destiny. They allowed me to move around the caves they lived in under supervision. Basic words, mostly commands I had to obey, became familiar. They took turns in getting me out. I still wondered at the reason for my captivity, at why they wished to maintain this state of affairs. I could have escaped at any point, but I was curious about these other people. Somehow or other, I felt it benefited me to observe them.

Afar, in the distance under the gray sky, I could hear the thundering ground below. The grunting monsters. A hazy memory of divine giants, otherworld intervention, fleshy delights.

Speak directly, look directly into his eyes. Give silent commands understood through chemistry, atmosphere, bodily language, bypassing, surpassing, verbal language. A kind word spoken in a cruel tone, a cruel world spoken playfully, What weighs the most?

True language is wordless. Communication goes on in every action. Every implication needs words almost not at all. Only a few can enhance, add flavor to, and extend the shared experience, the participatory creation.

A dance between me and the cruel one, the sadist, took place during these weeks.

Random strikes moved on to beatings, which I could withstand. Lacking a systematic mind, he was yet content only with hitting me. If this continued, it would scale, and I had to do something about it, or allow myself to play the willing role of victim. He had enough shortcomings. There were his leanings towards small acts of evil. The collecting animal body parts, always little ones, still bloodied. All clues to a mind caught mid-plunge.

Why protect the person who hurt you?

Rather than having a lost soul turn on you, make you the object of their sadistic daydreams come true, redirect their intent. Nullify them one way or another, by their own hand.

There are certain patterns, shapes, and sounds that such a mental disposition prefers. It chooses them even before he is aware of it. They become akin to the path of savoring destruction. A path they have unwittingly embarked upon.

Represented on a wall, or on a piece of paper, it will intrigue them. They will be drawn to it. And such mysterious faces will direct their state of mind. It directs their attention in different ways.

And so I drew one such pattern on the wall of my cell. It was large enough to be discernible by the targeted individual. It was also discreet enough that one could hide it from others.

You are not thinking, you are merely being logical.

A sadist will hurt others for their own pleasure. For kicks that require increasingly potent brews of cruelty. This much is true.

Twisted mechanisms that function within a mind like yours or mine, geared towards a different mode of living, of feeling, intent on satisfying urges of a different kind but employing the same type of neurology as any other human being.

Here was my bet. I could lead him to overt acts of blasphemy. I could to drive over an edge. The edge upon which his already insane proclivity hinged. When it became evident to his compatriots, then the group itself would get rid of him. His threat to me would disappear.

I assume many things. Things could go wrong. The justice imparted by the commander of the operational group is null when popular sentiment is not allowed to boil over. Like anything else, orchestration of a self-incriminating plot requires the deployment of certain personal resources. Use direct language and avoid the use of certain phrases. Every uttering, a calculated move on a chessboard.

The threat of coercion destroys resistance more than coercion itself. Threat causes worries, and initiates inner processes, as opposed to the act itself. Advanced mental models acknowledge that the pain of an event lies in its anticipation and its memory. The event itself happens in a moment and is soon gone, out of sight. So is the difficulty of an action. We fear we may not be up to the task.

So is the pain of effort. The exertion, we soon become accustomed to. We can surmount it by taking it upon ourselves to be at peace with the work that must be done to get what we want.

The eye forces the shape, it acts on matter.

How I view the person before me. How their voice sounds to my ears, whether good or evil, comes down to what I decide to think of them. If I had it in me, I could heal even the most despicable. Even individuals who mean me harm. Even if such harming had no reason except pleasure.

I could, I feel, if I chose to, eliminate them. How much would it serve me to go to such lengths for the supposed good? to do something for someone else that might end my life for the sake *the good*? Or, worse, to end up a pariah among those who fear the use of lethal force on principle?

Domineering, authoritarian energy fills my vessel. A transition into a being of short temper, impatience, and fast brutality ensues. Conviction transmitted at the end of fists. The art of knotting, balling bodies into limp bags to be thrown around. He ends up with his chest on the ground, out of air, a rag stuffed in his mouth. Moving the small nightstand out of the way, I show him the piece of art. Occult and occulted. Dripping dark dry red, cryptic symbols all around it, designed just for him. He fears it, just a little, and confusion makes ripe his mind for intrusion, for collection.

Has rapport been established? Undoubtedly.

We are now as close as we shall ever be. As any two humans can ever become. As any two have the right to be.

Through violence, the inextricable link between victim and perpetrator comes to terms. It establishes the purest dominance hierarchy. Leaving no doubt, no room for him to doubt.

The peace brought by a sadomasochistic arrangement is hard to explain to those in self-denial.

That peace which only certainty affords. The need for there to be a clear path, and a purpose, a firm commanding voice to forge ahead.

The human mind comprises an electrostatic field with frequency and amplitude. A determined configuration connected to and receiving transmissions from the universe. The shadows that he sees, others project onto him. These others are, in turn, the shadows he projects. A never-ending game of mirrors one cannot avoid. One utilized for better ends. For ends amenable to your own constitution and to your own views.

Such a predilection presupposes a person at least self-assured enough to not bow down before the exigencies of the myth of humility, the inborn burden of the slave and servant, and, instead proudly carry that flame which others call arrogance. Only in recognition of the self does the other also shine for what he truly is, as opposed to you. As something valuable because different. Something you would do well pay attention to. A kind of deference in its own right.

Thorough medical examination, including all body cavities, is administered by the facility doctor and team of nurses. He went through with it, I gather, after they found him communing with the enemy. They found him kneeling unconscious before a blood-drenched altar. One of the darkest type. That is where I had slipped.

I allowed them to involve me in my own attempt to divert the pervert into an act that would help me get rid of him. Now I was seen with a suspicion. A suspicion I had managed to avoid vaguely, if not artfully, during all past encounters. Now the tides had turned. I had to do something.

I had with me for an uncertain ally, in the best of cases, a maladjusted man. He was a twisted mental pattern raging and craving for suffering. He lusted after spikes of sensation that only cruelty and gore could fit. It was also a fire that no water could hope to quench.

Operations are meant to be carried out in ritualistic rather than insightful fashion. A certain amount of conflict is to be expected but is overcome by focusing on protocol.

My fellow prisoner, I tell him, you need not understand why we do things the way we do, what is important is that it works. It is only by putting it to the test that you will affirm or reject the truth of my words.

At this, he looked at me, too tired to feel or express the kind of suspicion that he probably felt he should express. His disheveled hair and bruised semblance was enough to make anyone wince, but staring deep into his eyes I could see rage stirring, flames kindled with the fuel of abandonment.

He said to me, you don't know what you've gotten yourself into. These people, they won't tolerate this sort of thing, the triangle, the circle, the strange symbols, and especially the blood. The blood is sacred to them, because of their book, you see.

The terror of violence at the hands of brutes and the common defenselessness of prisoners makes the affair all the more harrowing. In such cases, the only possible wisdom is to remain silent. And from a position of silence, you can observe better.

You can remove yourself from the equation. You stand aside as evens pass you by. You come to learn what true decision making is.

And so I tried. I tried to stare into his face, through his eyes and into his brain, with the hope of capturing within my own physiology what he was going through. It was terrifying, whatever was inside him. Confusing, too. I would have to hide, get out of his way, to avoid hurting him.

The smallest egos are the most aggressive, it has been said. I have no idea if this is true or not, but I have learned that control begins with tranquil awareness of a sense of flow, of appropriateness, and the prudence that comes with them. And so, I was quiet before this man who I thought so different from me in almost every respect. This man who smiles at me, a widening, knowing grin.

As I stare back at him with what I hope is my most neutral expression, a thousand other thoughts cross my mind. The body is the false scenery, it is only a channel for sensory experience. The components once and still thought to have been separate are layers of the same matter. That is, energy in fixed movement patterns.

I thought they were written in cipher. That the way the astral and the physical interacted differed only in mathematical calibration. That they could somehow collapse on top of one another. Soon I have disconnected from reality, thinking about reality. The moment, the fleeting opportunity, passes, and I have been dismissed.

He has turned his back to me, and is busy fixing and rummaging through his scant possessions. A dirty ruck sack, tattered and blackened beyond repair, holds all of his worldly possessions. I cannot help but be curious.

What are you looking at? says he, to which I can only shrug my shoulders.

I began the narrative by profiling, affecting related techniques, and inducing a meditative state in those listening. I can put pictures up, surround you with sounds, install feelings across your anatomy. I have done it before and I will do so again.

Patience and constancy make the brain and body yield to verbal cognition, the art of self-hypnosis. There is a point in our lives at which we must decide whether we will remain the helpless spectators of the circus of human life, of cruel nature, of an uncaring cosmos, or whether we will take the reins of our existence and conquer all that we can conquer. It comes down to the individual.

For too long, I thought mere humility, existing in the shadows, was the best way, to achieve and be out of the way. The way of the specter is not so bad. Especially if it is accentuated by proud markers of accomplishment, proofs to the universe, and to yourself. That you do hold all of the power you know you have inherited.

Inherited from whom?

From ancestors, some will say, but I am not so sure. The lines of attainment in the different worlds of the cosmos do not function the same, and any merit and power one gathers in the material realm can only translate into actualized power by jumping altogether from one genetic line into another.

Genetic lines may accrue wealth in the material world, but the value of the individual, provided he has discovered what he actually is, has a deeper source. I was born in the underworld to learn, mutate, and escape. Here on the surface, my kindness had only earned me condescension. And my silly attempt at a playful subterfuge backfired so that my physical existence was in danger.

Be careful not to rebuff him, otherwise rapport will be destroyed. A laboratory demonstration, the purest kind of light sends out a beam through an ideal pebble, an interference pattern of light and dark ripples onto a photographic plate.

A threat should be delivered coldly, skewing anger, with expressions of hostility, installing fear. Complex mechanical procedures, excellent engineers, and military technicians whose decisiveness, persistence and aggression are required, are but fools manipulated by the upper hierarchy. Lean back, sweetheart, be a good girl.

She receded into herself, into her deepest self. It would take many years before the outward immobility could be broken voluntarily, and not only at the behest of the overlord who trained her in the silent arts of killing and shackled her mind to his iron fist.

She recounted amid sobs what was done to her in the name of their religion. These holy men who held us captive for our transgressions. Their bloodletting was sanctioned, their violence sacred. Ours was a perversion.

That day, at that precise hour, I resolved to end his life. And so it was done. In the middle of the night, the thinnest wire cut into his larynx, and my hands bled, though cloth wrapped around them. Instantly, I felt alone, so alone.

It had always been like this with me. I sought others I despised, others I disliked, and tried my best to connect, to form a bond of love out of pity, sometimes out of self-pity. I never liked him, and yet he gave me much. Information, yes, but also a piece of his humanity, which was greater than mine.

His corpse soon attracted attention. In they came. Armed. Making noises of surprise. I laughed and smiled, unveiling a side that was true, though not altogether. And when they came in, two of them. Their leader stood outside cell. The saw wire was around the victim's neck.

The others tried to help, but my dying man's body danced between us, entangled in a waltz of death, the throes of an untimely passion. Too much drama for you who only hears the story, perhaps, but not for those who lived it, who died during the altercation.

We cut a path through the dry chilly wilderness, light warm cloth wrapped around us, she and I, hands stained with the blood of our erstwhile caretakers.

How long were you there for, her voice a soft rasp, About a few weeks after I came out of the ground. That was the extent of our conversation for many miles.

Only the blowing wind interrupted the sound of our footsteps. We had a wordless understanding, a common origin. I would not have at that point put it beyond her to slice my neck. Something called us both forward, into the mist, and away from the encampments, the villages, those who believed themselves the remnants of civilization. The cattle, at any rate, violent and petty, carrying out the wishes of a nameless god, one of many, who could not care less who was sacrificed for them.

In this universe of many faces, it boils down to that, who will you kneel to. Ignorance drove me as much as curiosity, the instinct declaring those who in the mountains made their temples and shrines to the absolute can only fit into a category of men capable of carving a path above and beyond. She held back what she knew, and I did not need to know.

I matched the rhythm of her steps, observed her shoulders, walking by her side, noting her inhales and making myself a shadow of hers, relaxing into it, gently breathing her in. No point thinking whether she might have ended my life, because she did not try to. She made no remark that could give rise to that suspicion. Not to these penetrating eyes nor this discerning mind.

The path I walk describes an inversion forcing the fragmentary into unity. It creates a mystical form that brings out what is hidden. It draws it from that which has no shape, a reunion of abstract possibilities.

Throughout detention, the prisoner must be convinced his destiny ultimately lies in the hands of his controller. Convinced that his absolute cooperation is essential to his survival.

The clear and starry night was made visible by an unseen hand. The multiple state where phenomena are realized instigates proclamations of desire. The need to search out and identify with a crooked finger scraping for an ideological compatibility is individualistic and self-centered. It has all to do with seeking acceptance.

She asked my name, I have no name, not anymore, at any rate. She accepted that answer. Names have no importance, no relevance to those who have shed their skins time and again. I tell myself she understood this. Perhaps she was only guided by her own wisdom, born as it was of suffering, part of the black light that surrounded her figure. Her cadaverous ruinous presence, wiry muscularity, with the eyes of a hawk. She moved, she prowled, it was her default mode of being, the destruction of temples, gouging the eyes of false prophets.

We shared food off the metal paraphernalia lifted from the burning houses we left behind, the memory of carnage still fresh in our minds. We made no distinction between the guilty and the innocent, whatever those words mean.

Beyond the halls of decency lies only the dichotomy of connection or disconnection. Whether one believes it or not, that is how the world appears to operate, not to speak of the uncaring cosmos. Her calloused hands, her terrible hands, and rough knuckles made me wonder how much of the great mother was still in her.

For he had been deformed, purposefully, cruelly, to atone for the sins of her ancestors. And yet, the twisted strength that she had been made to develop, the non-negotiability of her finesse, much needed in her line of devotional work, made impossible for her female lines, and curves to come out, even if in a form abhorrent to nature. The state of her body, incapable of reproduction, even at such a ripe age, probably not three decades in existence. Her face, an admixture of beauty and coarseness. Each and every one of them, indicators, hallmarks if you will, of the systematic ritual torture of the old ways.

Up to this point all has been relatively simple and easy to follow, involving perceptions that can be addressed through normal human consciousness. I am dedicated to change, modification, perfection, and social control, whatever the political, social, religious or institutional values of the system. It need not be real just yet, its energy can be absorbed by directly experiencing it, acting with it, as befits libido.

Thus, the indeterminate becomes determinate. As they age, others are forced away into nothing. Hence their need for offspring, the psychological need to multiply. But those of our kind seek to grow infinitely just as the cosmos does, the absolute, the gods, and fertility itself may be temporarily sacrificed on the journey.

The delusion of it, of course, is that more life can only beget more life, and it only depends on where that attention, that care, is dedicated. Ancient souls disguised in skins brought into the world, circles of forgetfulness, the lie of reincarnation, the diamond walls that crumble under heretical prayers.

I smile as I hear the echoes of their downfall, as we climb the steep slope with only the full moon to show us the way. She wanted it this way.

We were in sight of her objective early in the day, but she insisted. We must wait for the dark. For what I said, and her eyes pleaded, not menacing, for she had sensed, deep through her three brains, that I meant no harm, that I was in league with her, that I had no agenda except to help. It is what I wanted her to believe, and it was also true, because I made it true, on purpose.

Such is the decision taken with knowledge beyond the caprices of the automaton, that serves this and that, and one knows not what it is one is supposed to be, to want, to follow, to do and live. You choose and you do, you advance, and you choose again, you enjoy, you suffer, and you learn.

Every bit of knowledge, every reflection of your faceless being on the many faces of the world, the same moon reflected on all the watery surfaces, slightly different, in taste and hue, and in the voices that answer its appearance.

The entrance to the cave betrayed nothing of what it housed. Her excitement alone drew me forth. She could not stop smiling a wide grin, wide open eyes, mad and maddening, and I drank from that cup and felt ecstatically insane myself as well, I felt myself fall while standing. We are here, and we must go down, her voice a trembling whisper.

The ripples created upon the surface of the water preserved the moment instantly. The substance we feed ourselves pervades our domain. It incites a never-ending mutation. A defector feels his desires were not satisfied in his native lands. Unflinching honesty based on close and careful observation, congenial and compatible with the task at hand.

Representation is capable of encoding so much detail that even the lowest subjects can be examined with precision. He denies himself as the manifested cause, forgetting the light of that he is upon the physical space.

The return of all things bestial, the return to past times, false glory, elusive golden age plastered on the walls of ruins claiming to go back through time immemorial. All of these we passed, the voice calling from within the dark and stunted passage.

She laughed, she cackled, and soon we saw the flickering of flames ahead, atop torches. She moved fast, I did not see her, and I crouched to observe, moved along the wall. I heard grunts, bones and cartilage breaking. The closer I came the more I could see, the altar and the robed figures, the chained figure, bloodied and bludgeoned, the artwork of hell, the work of civilized sociopaths.

All of these she dispatched, and soon after the ritual victim. When all was said and done, when the rivers of blood did flow, she collapsed beside the altar, weakened by her effort, feats no normal human could have withstood.

Childlike in her movements, in her gestures, in her helplessness, she made to grab the chains that held the corpse of the tortured woman, still warm, mangled. Something old stirred within me, and I acquiesced to her desires, not out of pity nor out of decency, for I had nothing of either.

It was truth, the cleansing truth, that spoke across eons of time, and brought liberation of the human spirit, of the dead ones who made it, of Herakles the first and only god of the Hellenes. I had studied this, and so I put two and two together in my mind. In practice, I only followed what seemed right, what I had come to know as honor, a mixture of intuition filtered through reason, not given, not delegated, not mediated by any authority, but evaluated through experience. Nothing was more appropriate, more honorable, or needed than for me to take her out of that dark place of black stone and red fire and blood, out into the open, where the wind our friend would tell us what to do, and carry us off where it would.

If we let it.

She weighed nothing, or close to nothing, to a body familiar with greater loads above and beyond what this poor woman could possibly mean. She was soon breathing normally as I set her under the shade of a tree, which by noon next day proved itself the best choice give the surroundings.

I washed her wounds with the cleanest fabric I could find, and with water I brought up several miles from the closest river, the largest of the hand-held containers the late cultists stashed in the cave down below us. Towering abysses and sacred woods lay exposed by the high sun of noon, telling of a vibrant gamut of possibilities open to us, or to me at any rate, for I do not think there was much more for her, other than ecstatic revenge. I did not blame her captors, nor did I blame her.

It was as the cosmos was, and they, we, were all just creatures in it, finding our way, finding the ways, in which to move, trapped or not, according to each one's make and preference. But, as I said before, my sense of honor drew me to her, to her cause, according to my experience and instinct, no matter what the momentary emotions did to my perception.

In the soft light of the afternoon, I caught sight too, of the many small tattoos that dotted her skin here and there, not very obvious on her brown tanned skin in the middle of the night in a cell, but quite obvious now when I bathed her. I was surprised enough that she let me bathe her from the top of her head to the tips of her toes. She was glorious, in the way an assault rifle can be glorious, except she also had a soul.

Marked creativity tends to displace or sublimate sexual needs in those with high intelligence. Life and death are very dear, indeed, but only as poles in an energized dynamic, and not as the sources of meaning the commoner, the self-made prisoner, takes them to be. Adopting the tone of an understanding father or older brother makes a great difference.

You know the facts.

He feels a little guilt about his lack of social versatility. We move differently, touching, smiling, avoiding, knowing it is all a game, yet too lazy, too out there, to take it all too seriously. Only those successfully traumatized and matured enough can then understand alien ones, the ones who do not fit, for they are also made unfit by their suffering, and by overcoming their suffering they are also made stronger.

The firmest, most capable alliance forms thereof, and nothing may stop them. The signs upon her body were in the secret writing system of an old sorcerer who stole a mirror of black stone from a great temple in another continent, brought over by conquerors as worthy as any other, maligned only for the color of their skin in later times.

Slowly, she came back to her senses, and she smiled, for the carnage was to her the sole purpose of her existence, the purveyor of meaning and drive, of narrative and sexuality. And yet, beneath all that confused, weaponized nervous system, that honed capacity to destroy, there was kindness and empathy, in a consciousness still dormant, or a hollow machine was she, for she observed nothing but only preyed. Now, she enjoyed my ministrations which sought only to clean, to heal, to activate. And while I did so, my mind took stock of the situation.

You tasked me to provide an assessment of its mechanics and ultimate practicality, of the crimes in their forests, of the ghostly sisters, and as a result whatever I say is likely to mirror the cultural milieu of the organization.

As a lover, my tongue is bound to erupt with the language of roses, arriving at a singularity, breaking down Aristotelian concepts, passing from mere potentiality to action. I am conscious energy in infinity, overlaying everything, and through me renewal of the cosmos is experienced in the promiscuity of countless observers.

By sundown she was asleep again and all I had managed to trap and skewer were two squirrels. Fresh water from the river proved a godsend and was enough to nourish me aside from the smallest bit of meat.

I let myself drift off under the blanket of stars, copious, and I could not believe there had been a time when the earth was so polluted with light that you could not see the stars like I did, nor that you could have your eyes so ruined by incorrectly dialed artificial life, for all human life is artificial, that you would need instruments of all sorts to even be able to catch the divine light from the travelers above.

She stirred, awoke. She fed on the bits of critter I left for her. She quenched her thirst with a litter of fresh water and asked for more. I pointed her in the direction of the river, telling her to be careful, warning her of the places where she would need to go slower, and of the strange animals I had seen on my way there, and off she was.

I did not hear her leave, nor did I catch the fall of her naked feet on the stone, as intently as I paid heed. The remaining warmth of the sun laid trapped in the stones upon which I lay, contrasting comfortably with the cool air of the mountain, and I wonder if I would be able to see the ship among the stars that night, the innermost sanctum across the sky, the one no mere human eyes could see. In the distance, thunder.

In the air, the unmistakable smell of danger.

The sign of doom.

Somehow, even to my trained perception, that cave, the rites enacted therein, reeked of danger, of danger intangible yet personified. Had I been reading a report, I would have asked myself why the members of the expedition had not taken refuge within.

Laying here, that horrid place well within my sight, I understood we had to put a great distance between us and it, or something would come for us. Childlike paranoia had not assaulted my brain ever since I was a toddler. The phenomenon was well-understood. I faced something new, a darker foe, the incarnation of an ancient fear come alive was about.

The action of desire throws us into a possible world, a new panorama to attempt, a channel for revelation. A single vibrating energy field makes up the human being. Joint power sooner or later leads to recriminations and strained relations between participants. Unilateral power is the only answer. Doing what you consider to be useful, making it through to the end, utilizing the daydream without escaping in a frivolous manner, appreciating your thoughts, this missive from the center of yourself, uncomfortable because silencing, the untouchable heart.

As she exhaled for the last time in my arms, I inherited a part of her. Surely, not the breaking of chains, for that belonged to me already. I did not need any one to come and teach me to rebel against the status quo.

The ground under my feet turned red, and so did the sunsets, drastic in their fiery brushstrokes, moving canvasses made of irreplaceable moments that would never once again occur, and which only presented themselves thus to me and to me alone.

The landscape passed me by, with its blue mountains and brown deserts, its mists and its comets. She was alive long enough to give me instructions for an improvised mummification. Being put on this earth who knows for what reason,

I had long ago made up my mind to take what I was offered and do to the best of my ability what most resonated with my instincts. It was a painstaking process, and for weeks I struggled to gather and enact the procedures she asked of me, knowing full well that the result would be far from those of the ancient priests. She cared not. Even in her madness she was capable of impressing upon my mind the idea that all that mattered was that a kernel of her physicality was preserved.

As I listened to her and repeated them back to her to verify the accuracy of my memory, she asked a more dire question. Would I carry her with me to the Temple Beyond the Veil.

Where is that?

Just keep walking down this mountain path and keep to the Eastward path until you reach The Great Plains, then turn Northward, and be ever ready to encounter evil.

Energy creates projecting or expanding, a living pattern most easily understood by visualizing a bowl full of water. It is also important to maintain liaison with different groups within the region and abroad. To precipitate the desired paranoid panic reaction you will have to fight an impulse to stop suddenly when you recognize their vulnerability and become yourself an object to their hostility. The gate and connection is the profaned body made pure through rebirth.

Wrapped in clothing and dried up, her body weighed even less than it had in life. The marks that we had agreed would be made on the cloth that contained her remains had their artistic charm, and that was enough for me despite not having an inkling of what they meant. Their aesthetic itself created a wave of electricity through my body and, to my senses, the immediate surroundings. I kept these in mind, their curvilinear figures, and how content she had felt in making these, as if they made all the difference in the world.

I drew more and more energy from the memory, and from my awareness of their existence on the treasure I carried. It became a matter of ritual for me to stare at the symbols covering the bundle that was her while I rested under the shade of some straggling tree, or behind a rock that served as shield against the cruel sun.

Beyond space but limited to a specific location in the state of infinity, there but without a sense of area, without limit with respect to the fundamental, primal power existing in being. The empress presents herself.

What can you possibly control?

When did you learn your manners and from whom?

Crusader and advocate, accepting only of those with similar attitudes and tastes, the blackened body made ready for breaking. The universe is dependent on the vivisecting relation between the ocean and the myriad drops that form its body.

Night after night I dreamed of the authoritarian matriarch. She had only come to me a few weeks after I had mummified my female friend. Long after the distant spires of a great construction came into view.

We were not quite within view of the Great Plains, at least I did not think so, for I guessed I would know what such a terrain should look like. I had never lain eyes on the place I was looking for, neither had I ever seen a reproduction of its image in painting or photography.

Her body was bruised, not deceased, but dead in life, dead but dreaming, and in her dreaming she invaded my space. I asked what it was she wanted, but she would not answer, her eyes only glowed and her hair floated as if we were under water. The intense scarlet of her scaly suit was aesthetically pleasing, but I was not at all into the interpretation of such symbols, neither did they seem relevant to me.

For in each and every case, the answer to questions lie deeper than in the etymology and history of a word or a figure. The answer almost always lies in an emotion linked to a memory, in a sensation and a tension housing a terror to be confronted, an unresolved mystery begging you to open the door and move through the darkness without shining the cursed light, shunned reason.

Tell the old lady to shut up.

I am more interested in what a person should be than in trying to understand where the answer lies. Mysticism, religious fervor, and intense dedication to theoretical and philosophical concepts are the common manifestation of those who are anxious about their inability to control sensuality. So did the edifice of the intruder, the predator, crumble, for my will was greater than hers and far beyond anything she had ever met.

Either I was deluding myself into thinking the agent of chaos that confronted me in the twilight realm was in truth an independent being, or I was making great strides in the direction of conquering my inner cosmos. What really mattered was that I was gaining unprecedented control of the world that I could perceive. That is, of all of the world, from my point of view.

As long as you are always in control of your immediate surroundings, you are omnipotent, or close enough to it. She flew back, through the mirror, behind one of the waterfalls in the complex of waterfalls in one of the floating globes that I had come to explore time and again leaving my denser body behind.

I avoided the city, now in full view. The red tops of its spires one more warning, one more sign of danger, that I was to heed if I was going to retain consistency and keep the inner urgency demanded of my present circumstances from weakening. Even a great distance away, though within sight, my nose could distinguish the abundance of notes hanging in the air telling of an incredible richness of origins and creativity, of a land concerned primarily with momentary pleasure.

The price of that emphasis comes in the further and further abstraction of deities, enthroning a great figure beyond all human experience to counterbalance the endless and meaningless commerce that fills their experience. These things and more, I came only to know a long time after, but I make an effort of writing them here so that my alien experience does not also alienate my reader, so that you may understand and enjoy in a knowing way, different from what I experienced when the primary memories were formed.

The steep mountainside greeted me and the pain of the ascent was fuel for my soul, the burning sensation of accomplishment, just enough to make you feel alive, though not so much that you cannot go on. Balance in all things. The measure of the contents of your soul, the compensations that from a young age have made you irresolute, that have stopped you from becoming all you could be, leaving the damned city aside and its decadence, its bigotry hidden as tolerance, making use of children's souls to elevate its mighty towers, a testament to purposeful suffering.

How much of this demonic operation will you go along with, and by how much are you willing to delay your own ascendancy because you do not feel ready?

All of these thoughts circled through my mind, carrying the mummy with me, my beloved mummy, everything I had in the world, and the sum, nay, more than the sum of all the relationships I had ever had, our astral bodies bonding, crossing, fusing, and not letting go of each other, hands holding in the purity of a love beyond death, triumphing over death. The scent trail, vague as it was, extended before me toward my destination, and beyond.

Reverse the origin and you will find the path I walk upon, the manifold in favor of the ability to see and experience plurality. The governess extended her black hand across eons of time and space, all lies of course, she's here with me, she's always been here with me, and I shall always tread the lacerated earth with heavy boots.

The sword that once belonged to a sorcerer in the ashes of a blackened castle shone brightly in my dreams. Screams up on the hill feed into the blood of my legs, and excited to see the scene of torture that so awfully rips my soul apart the last of the obstacles is overcome. The violent suffering of another, the source of pain and pleasure in one's own soul, the battering ram against the long abandoned doors of my inner mansions.

Before me, the pale moonlight deters more than it aids my failing eyes, orbs full of tears, rivers of compassion watering the moss and dust underfoot. She laughs, she of the stars. I hear the echo of her cackle return to me from the stone protrusions surrounding us.

Even in death she warns me.

Security services work with methods to melt resistance, contriving ways in which target subjects can be lawfully detained. They will employ the most forbidden of arts, hidden away in tomes, thought eradicated by the fire of witchfinder generals, returned to the gaping maw of nothingness whence they fell through the womb of atrocious conception.

I thought of her who from the stars once came, as she stood before the congregation so many moons ago, lifetimes ago it seemed, traumatic waves, tides of solitude, shrouding her eyes from the blessing of my consuming impulse.

The abomination then stood, struck an immortal wound upon both our souls, her sordid mating call, an ever-opening flower weaving suffering, of broken knees and scraped tongues, the sound of millions of cultists dreaming of her, though never in such vivid glory.

He is extremely impatient with distraction, not a particularly bright boy or pretty, and quick to fury. The treacherous memory assailed me, the time to be cruel was at hand, to slash off the tentacle, the suckles threatening to rip my scalp clean. The young man claiming to have visions, his body cut open for biopsies, behaviorist obsessions, sexual perversions, disguised and excused in the name of science, seeking the meaning of both his power and his process, his extended perception, ancient times before we killed them all.

A return to vaster planes of existence, to gigantic bodies that soared across the multiverse, and who only incarnated in these fleshy contraptions to render the path harsher and so alchemically viable.

So it was conceived, so it has been done. And now the neutered harpy, this winged female being, this impossible being, crazed cries flying through the air, death towering inescapable.

The term matter as a solid substance is misleading. It does not exist. There are only degrees of energetic movement. The universe is an unstable cube, an unfinished, on-going creation.

Whence came she who thus wove threads across the matrix of my crucified body? You brought me here, or I am here because of you, to tell you many things without speaking them. The lava flows will soon cool and the sword of pre-eval Night will be within your grasp.

Her features both birdlike and womanlike contorted hysterically, the wings behind her arms letting off plumage as she gestured to and fro. She looked into my eyes and smiled, or her eyes did, as far as I could tell.

Why would I need such a weapon and what do you know of my quest?

Do not assume anything, know the pertinent statutes, and review them periodically. The quest is not yours originally, but is given to you. I am but the messenger of your salvation. We know you are lost, seeking only a way to bring your friend back to life. We know also that she lives, after her own manner, and that your crude mummification will suffice for the time being. Though not for as long as it could, if you were to come across better technologies, higher purposes. I have spoken to you for entire days, while you stood dazed staring through me. You also ignore that you summoned me just as I am. However I seem to you, sound to you, is your doing and yours alone. The time has come for you to leave your burden aside. Cut it down, through it.

I watched her with great disgust. A knot in my throat, a perpetual knot that only loosened when every reason, memory and future was let go.

What is this sword you speak of, and what are you getting at now? You suggest the burden I physically carry is something to set aside, to forget, and to go on with my life.

She interrupted, raising her wings, rippling muscles and colored feathers offering a macabre vision.

You are unrealistic and inappropriate. You demand. Yet you mean what you say. So called states of matter are actually variances in human consciousness, fecund matter in the midst of the void. While you carry that thing beside you she is tied to you, especially after what you have done to it. The rites you have undergone. The binds of intention you sealed with the help of the stones and the moon, to whom you spoke that night. The sword you will need to bring her back, but with the sword her dissected remains will yield onto you the precise anchoring point of her being. It is that kernel which you must then take up to an ancient cathedral.

I laughed at her, not wanting to let her know she had me in her grasp. The flesh, kindled by the fire of impulse, was ready to go. But the calculations of my brain, the incessant flow of ideas, of remembrances of history, treason recorded in books, fed a different attitude.

She saw through me. Her raucous voice echoed once more among the rocks. Sarcasm, cynicism, and bitterness are characteristic of those who are brutally frank, by their own admission.

It is the shield of the inept at heart. Having so declared, she came at me, talons at the ready. I lunged and rolled to my right. Taking refuge behind a rock I sought to reposition myself in order to take the offensive against the miserable creature. The long knife should do well enough, had I something to put between it and me.

Alas, when I looked over the rock she was gone. I heard neither the beating of her wings nor caught sight of her flying away.

Unsure of whether the danger had passed, I kept to the rocks, examined the skies. There was no indication that she had left, nor that she remained in the vicinity. Hours passed. Fatigue demolished the bastions of my anguish. Sleep crept over the walls, and I flew out the gate in dreams troubled and chaotic.

I was then in a village, Arabic and Hebrew, as far as I could tell, were spoken. I said Shalom and moved past. Up dirt roads, little houses. Modern vehicles and rundown houses. I walked for hours, in the mud. Until at last I came upon a road, under the rain, that I recognized. With great expectancy I took the path uphill and soon viewed the red brick walls of several buildings. Religious or otherwise, a place of learning, of freedom.

All this I felt, no one spoke to me, nor had I conscious knowledge of where I was. The upsurge of happiness that came over me pushed me back, closed my eyes there, and opened them here. I awoke in the late hours of the morning, back at the hilltop near the ruins where the harpy and I had conversed.

A centripetal force intervenes, exploiting the melting pot of souls. Human consciousness transcends language, this is the stigma of its occult connotations.

Within security limitations, circulate bio-data to receive filtered feedback on the prisoner, right brain intuitive insights of the concepts involved leading to construction and application. I came here to celebrate all that is unfair, the essence of the negative way. If the room is free of distractions, without a result, then a vertical thrust remains the only viable option. The only prisoner here is me. The cell and the iron bars imagined, the door is open.

I put my faith aside long ago, though I never quite let go of it. Words were the problem. Faith in our cybernetic core. The link remained intact, but one mustn't try too hard at that. The ways in which the god returns to earth, the roots that extinguish all manner of alien life that comes too near. It can be too much to bear for some. It is an ecstasy. An ecstasy in panic.

While you are busy, away in your thoughts, said she, time passes us by.

The clouds parted and lightning flashed as I turned around astounded. As she was tied to my back, turning around left me looking at the barren ground and the grass tufts in front of me. Yesterday she was still, dead by the old way of looking at things. I knew why I was carrying this mummy. I knew that somehow it might be possible to bring her back. To enjoy her company once more, to learn from her madness. Now her voice came unexpected, and unexpected as well was how reassuring, comforting it was from beyond the grave.

I took her off my back and unwrapped her face, I wanted to see her face and mouth at least. She was dry, still. It was impossible for her to have spoken. Yet I heard her voice.

You will keep hearing it as long as you want me around you. Otherwise dump this body, or cut it in half as the harpy told you.

Her voice was in my head. But impervious as I was to the idea of going mad, I decided to welcome the experience, even as I welcomed the lonesome crags and howling twisted trees ahead.

Go on, said she, what are you waiting for?

These halls you have hankered after even in dreams, that seemed to give you all you wanted, are you ready to let them go and seek further aloft?

Understand you now she said this in my mind, for the little wrapped body moved not, no gesticulations came to me from where she was. For I knew she must be somewhere. I imagined it was on a misty grassland suffused in violet light that she would be, ambling about. To a certain degree, if so I thought, so it must have been. Somewhere, sometime.

As to what was going on here and now, right in front of me, I can only bear witness to what I experienced and not to what I was supposed to have experienced. I cried on that dried corpse, dry by my own hands, under her direction.

I slide into my dusty boots, gray and torn with wear, they have always been a little too big for comfort. But that is how I like them, feeling unsafe in footwear that fits too tight. A specter in the rocks waves its bony finger at me, beckoning me.

The scholarly guests at the red-bricked buildings pay me no heed, and instead went about their businesses, each of them, grasping their books, their papers, not hurried but content, curious, full of dreams. I move forward and she smiles, I have already forgotten her name. She is wrapped to my body, on my back, and yet I know she smiles.

Let's go beyond this conversation, this discussion on whether or not I am the cancer you must extirpate from your life. The thoughts that fly through your mind are just that, ideas and possibilities. They need not reflect nothing that matters. The things that truly matter are those that happen to you. Focus on that. You have come this far, a place you thought you would only see in dreams, and now it is time to move forward. You may someday do the impossible, to bring me back to life, through your preserving and restitution of this physical anchor. Move forth I say and tarry not any longer.

Aren't you just arguing in favor of your own interests. I say this even as I go up the path, closing the door of the hip-high wooden fence behind me. And even as I say it, the cold wind upon my face, the placid rays of morning sunlight cut through the mist, and I take one step after the other. There is nothing left to say. Voices beckon, the voices of those housed in my sinews, in the sparkling fires of my nerve circuitry.

What violence I must do I must inflict upon others and not myself, and only with great pleasure. I think it won't come to that, replied she at this thought. Now she was in my head. But it will not always be like that. You do not know that. That is true, but somehow I think that having a properly functioning body again will bring our telepathic connection under control. Well, we'll see.

The cheese wheel I took from the kitchen is fresh, not too salty. They do not have these up north, certainly not in the underground dungeons I escaped. Over there it is all about function. How does this flavor factor in, and they do take into account a nuanced variety of emotional and sensual factors. But the further I got into a position of power, such as it was, the more I understood the dual use of ecstasy and panic.

Some pleasure is good, at the right time, but not all the time. Pleasure is accentuated by the long barren spans in between each delectable session. Not a victim, but a product, the result of generations of research, of conscious evolution. And it was the warm bread and the nurturing feeling instilled by the earthly sustenance that brought me closer to essence.

Are you still getting that sword, the ancient sword of night the harpy spoke about? Yes. It might come in handy. There are tasks ahead. She had suggested before, independently of the idea of splitting your mummy.

Blue thunder parts the sky, through the gray cotton cloud, the skies laughed with her and I heard her not again. I talked and talked, and was surprised her voice was gone, or she was gone?

The land alone, the sound of the wind, filled my field of perception. Every rock I passed I counted an accomplishment, and from behind one sometimes a curious animal would pop out. A badger here, a bird there. It really did not make sense that so many of these creatures would make their homes right by the road. I tried not to let that bother me, now that she had fallen silent again.

There, by the river, I set down my load. It looks more deceased than ever before. Lighter, I would say. I shake it to see if anything inside it is loose, not very scientific, but I wanted to find out, to relieve this burden of unknowing, the doubt that clung like an anvil tied with a rope around my neck.

The light blue blanket she was wrapped with matches the grays and greens, the browns and similar hues of our sequestered surroundings. Night falls fast, I have got nothing to eat. All that remains is to sleep, to hunt in dreams, to let it fly, to loosen the last screws that scare away the genius. I give myself wholly to the current that takes away souls from their bodies at night. At the last moment I am resolved to remember, to reject oblivion, to go into the darkness of my own free will. And so my dreams conform. As I explore another cavern in search of prey, they appear with their machines, executioners in the service of the governess. I am too experienced to think this is only a dream, to let it all go and tell myself it too shall soon pass. Waking, I gather everything I possess, everything that remains, and I go my own way.

Consumed by thoughts, I mechanically move forward, the mud providing the one and only textural distraction to my short-sighted attention, my reduced area of perception. The plan has not been adhered to. Chastisement procedures, applied by the invisible organization, will not be suitable for me. The programming has effected its effect. I understand or, more precisely, my flesh knows, what matters, what does not, that the mortifying of it serves only to encode through a certain flavor of intense sensations.

On we move, as the rain, a little drizzle, comes to greet us. Mud starts to form under my worn boots, and I try to stand on rocks as often as I can help it. The warmth of her dead body against my back, what little weight it has, makes no sense.

She's dead, but dreaming.

The massive underground carved out places of worship that we designed, and by we I of course mean the organization under the governess, of which I once was quite the enthusiastic particle, came to my mind, as if solidifying out of the clouds, their shapes so subject to interpretation. A chill travels up my spine. Instead of letting it fizzle away, I catch it, defuse it so that it extends, thins out, and covers my skin like a blanket. I am here, I am always here, forever and ever.

In certain societies women are viewed as inferior, a divergent cluster that is overtly sensual, while men are inhibited. They have acquired a conscience and a sense of social responsibility that hides their extreme self-centeredness. The role of resonance is that of identification, but requires the achievement of physical quietude in order to be subject to alteration.

The personal discovery that such a state of quietude leads to the resurgence of an ancient will led me to understand the organization tyrannically functioned at the expense of the vast ignorant mass, for the benefit of the few who were expected, at some level, to rebel, to escape the system of directed pressures.

I had been led by some invisible hand from one situation to another, so that even my accusers and my captors could not ponder why I was being kept in a bureaucratic limbo, outside of the usual processing channels, why my odd behavior triggered removal and reallocation, whereas outright opposition should have otherwise demanded swift termination or at the very least banishment.

Yet for all the talk of awakening, I have made more progress by following the impulses of my viscera, jumping into the unknown, justifying emotional bonds, all of which are hardly commensurate with reason and knowledge. For I reject that doctrine that talks of a knowledge without reason, bestowed upon the individual by mysterious and unseen forces that he or she can never quite identify. I who have jumped from one body to another, retained my identity, and returned to a version of my original vehicle, there and back again as one might say, I cannot be blamed for close mindedness.

Doubt, the touchstone of reason, is all I ask in return for adventurousness. It is strange how complete abandonment of all previous affiliation, the cutting of ties to associations that procured safety nets, brings liberation.

A king is a king who is safe through his power to deflect danger and exact retribution. He who cowers under foreign protection will only ever be a slave by their own choice.

Now the open country below us spells silent destruction, of soul and body, and up ahead, the caves. They did not seem like much. I heaved and panted, and the thought of finding great treasure in those inconspicuous entrances filled me with a thrilling sensation. Childlike, would be a way of describing the state. Soon, however, the adult kicks in, I stop. It is time to assess the possible dangers. I hear footsteps. I hear laughter.

Good morning, and god bless you.

It is a minister who speaks, black hat covering his eyes from my sight. It's a steep way up to the caves. Indeed they are, I answer. I come here every few weeks. I hesitate to give any answer. I am, after all, in search of a sword, an object I presume I must loot, though I hoped to avoid confrontation.

He moves faster than me, decrepit as he seems, smiling, glasses reflecting the light of day so that I never once see his true eyes. He grins, and moves faster, and faster up the hill. Impossibly fast. Like a wolf.

Come my child, tarry not for the time is nigh. I follow under the presumption of his ignorance and of my own power to obtain the upper hand. He will take me somewhere, since he at least knows where he is going, roughly in the same direction I must, as far as I can tell.

The way of action, of all great extremes, can be bent towards the loyal and dedicated following of a beneficial creed with little use for heretics and disbelievers. Self-discipline with anxiety and tension, pained screams that ring shrill, emotional involvements across virgin territory, the choice to survive or let go.

A lack of understanding that hardly calls for irreverence, a lack of training and experience in the applied techniques, all raise the question of termination. Cutting through means cutting down, to act and observe, to recalibrate, to keep throwing oneself in the midst of the next experience, adjusting, learning, growing, that is the path of fire, not the most glamorous but the most efficient.

The path of action.

That is all I knew and understood, after all those years of reclusive training, of channeled energy inflicted on the will of others in the service of some greater, inscrutable purpose. I felt the excitement, the physical sensation of tingling, waves, indicator of a state and, if harnessed correctly, precursor to opening of the gate of possibility.

Right on the cave entrance, a monument, a cross with detail, texture as of woven textiles upon it, a loop on top, not quite a cross, perhaps an ankh, maybe both, maybe neither, certainly resembling what I had seen in books not neither.

The minister looked at me, for I thought he was a minister, dressed in a long black cloak of the kind one would wear, and affecting that demeanor that only those totally at ease in their sure sense of destiny can exude. He smiled and now I could see his eyes, his hat off and a glistening brow, a face wet with sweat from the abnormal display of athletic ability, so fast and strange anyone else would have dismissed it in confusion or panic. Not I, who traced his details with my eyes, who waited for my body to plunge me into cold or light a fire in me, signals of one extreme or the other from a world I could only dimly grasp directly, but in which my being, as well as yours, is steeped, submerged, like a fish in a body of water.

Hostile penetration has always been, and remains, the most delectable method, beloved and preferred by all seasoned practitioners. The highly effective parish priest clasps his hands together in the air and brings them back behind his head. Remember to spell the difference between success and failure, select and use the correct techniques.

He does poorly, tends to concentrate in specialized fields, feels that what he has done, no one can undo. I never did well in school, he starts with me alone as audience, but I rose through the ranks through being good at obtaining sacrifice for the altars, for not flinching at the butchering of the lamb nor its procuring from the flock, something that is already too much for the majority to bear.

He unsheathes a blade and looks down at it, looks at me, more of a machete than a gladius, he swings, and I jump back, let myself slide down the dirt of the mountain, I hear him laugh behind me. I do not perceive his mortal plunge, only the fierce cry of his voice.

Presenting a conceptual model, the relative position of the universal hologram can be seen as a self-contained spiral. There is no such thing as the antithesis of time, as time is but a life adjustment achieved through considerable rebellion against God. The phallus is the vibrating axis around which the world turns, loyalty to a long-established dependency. It is the black rock at the center, magnetizing, amplifying desires transmitted right into the brains of all prey, human and alien.

KOSMOKRATOR

A primer for modern esoteric practice

Whoever declares himself to be God, let him come and finish this corner, and then all shall know he is a god.

Primary Practices

Correctly choosing the primary practices is an area of concern for anyone seeking to develop their overall capacities; by this we mean those of us seeking breakthroughs in the nature of human capacity itself above what is popularly touted as elite in sports or scholarly achievement. The primary practices would perhaps be different for people at different stages in their life, but not for reasons of social expectation.

Within the circles of people like us, who seek attainment beyond what is mundane or merely human, there is no separating the old from the young. On the contrary, what we may find to be primary practices are certainly largely overlooked in conventional education and culture so that young people would benefit from them as much as the old. Nevertheless, because we are agents rebelling against the overarching education and culture, we may also be taking for granted the positive aspects and skills we have developed as a result of having been brought up inside the system.

First suggestions

ANY PRACTICE THAT AIMS at the total development of the human element must take into account both the physical encasing in which we exist, and the non-physical element. For those of a materialistic bent, the term non-physical need not mean soul or ethereal force in any religious or esoteric sense. The nonphysical element of the human being refers simply to the experienced reality of our identity not being coeval with the body, either in part or in whole. Nobody experiences themselves as the brain nor even the nervous system.

This is why we talk about the body and its parts as *belonging* to us, as material possessions. Fans of by-now-debunked linguistic theories might want to argue that we think this way as a result of linguistic patterns we use. Unfortunately, this language-as-primary theory has taken root in the education system even as neuroscientists (or any person with the capacity for independent judgment) had early on realized it was invalid. One only has to look at the fact that no human group, no matter the language they use, will identify the individual with the body.

As a side note, identification of thinking with language, and of individual identity with the body, which go hand in hand, is a thin construct defended by a tiny minority of people bent on making strict materialism the dominant worldview. Like all imposed worldviews against the way of truth they suffer a common obstacle: if you try to impose something false, the falsehood will fail to take root completely, and old notions will keep growing anew everywhere like weeds in the garden of deception. It is precisely this that makes necessary the huge indoctrination machine extant in most developed countries. Against such fairy tales in all realms of knowledge, truth keeps propping up when *you pay attention to your senses* instead of looking for meaning or correctness according to a given framework or model.

With regards to physical disciplines, the body needs sleep, water, nutrition, recurrent exposure to sun and open spaces (both for eye and brain health), short bouts of strain when strength is exercised, and, most elusively, *correct use*. Correct use refers to proper movement patterns and coordination. These depend on a simple understanding of joint and muscle structure, pausing between activities to allow the nervous system to reset, and in the all-too-overlooked *listening to the body*. Listening to the body is very simple: if it hurts, if it is uncomfortable, it is probably wrong (in this instance, at this time, in such a way, etc.).

Listening to the body applies directly to all of the physical disciplines as well as to the nonphysical ones.

The beginning of all nonphysical discipline is, of necessity, nervous system discipline. At its most basic level is the ability to be non-reactive, as much as possible. Choosing to remain silent, immobile, despite input from the surrounding environment and the mind. Willing not-to-do anything, which excludes entertainment and distractions, concentrates on enhancing perception by only receiving incoming signals and observing their pathway through our bodies.

This deceptively simple, and oftentimes excruciatingly painful, practice is the beginning of self-knowledge and what in Buddhist nomenclature is referred to as the Eightfold Path. Most important of these eight elements, from the point of view of a true Westerner, is *right action*. From the discipline of the senses, and of the mind, will start to become manifest a plethora of subtle signals the extent and credibility of which only the individual experiencing them can judge.

Presuppositions

ONE ASSUMES THAT THE person is able-bodied and retains a manner of freedom of movement and decision making. Being able to make use of time and at least a basic amount of resources in their own terms, that is, possessing a modicum of freedom, is a prerequisite to development. Otherwise, priority should bend entirely to the acquisition of the perceived level of liberty that will allow the leeway necessary for the individual to pursue their true desire (the discovery and development of which is a journey in its own right).

We also assume that the person undertaking these disciplines will have the predisposition to get results without the need to cling to a narrative or aesthetic path to the detriment of their individual reality and survival. Martyrs, heroes, saints, ideologues, idealists, psychos and other archetypes with suicidal tendencies are likely not suited to a path that will continually unveil that *what you believe is wrong* in a never-ending sequence that stops only when one realizes that *believing is a delusion*. Believing, of course, includes active non-belief. The *negating position* is as much a belief as the affirming one.

That is not to say that each person cannot have and indeed indulge in their preferences, to their pleasure and ecstasy. A person with a developing ear for their inner voice will gravitate to a highly individualized path, composed of things that call out to them. However, it is necessary that these things are not merely decorative; this, the heart will also tell, for when in balance and in contact with the rest of reality, something entirely superfluous will be perceived as nauseating. But, of course, these are the assumptions we make regarding the individuals approaching the practices and heuristics advocated herein.

Individual priorities

WHAT AN INDIVIDUAL will choose to do, within the parameters described above, and on top of such a foundation, will differ with respect to interest and need. For instance, someone suffering from chronic physical discomfort in the joints, fatigue in the lower back, and so on, might be well advised to look first for solutions in that area. They might be called first to look into the Alexander Technique, which is all about posture correction towards what is natural for the human body in general and the proportions of the practitioner. From then on, a regimen of basic strength conditioning, mobility and displacement (i.e. walking, trekking, jogging, and so on) might be suitable. These are things we should all be partaking in, but we are calling to the reader's attention that investigating and developing them would be an enveloping first priority for those who recognize a sub-optimal use of their physical bodies.

Someone who has suffered throughout their life from a progressive worsening of the eyesight and eye health in general would be well advised to give eye care some attention. Mainstream resources as well as non-mainstream sources are worth looking into. In the latter classification, there is the Bates Method, which focuses on the idea that many people suffer from myopia or even astigmatism because of the *wrong use* of the eye. The idea here is that through correction of habits, the person can improve their eyesight as the health of the eye improves. The precise theory behind the Bates Method revolves revolves around the function of the muscular structure around the eye, and how our voluntary control can affect it. While decried by ophthalmologists since its inception as a fraud in the early twentieth century, it has never ceased having a hardcore following of people who claim to have found great relief by applying the Bates Method's exercises. It is worth noting that no appreciable niche industry has grown around the Bates Method, and its support and survival comes from advocates who read the original book and continued to share its principles.

People who struggle with sleep, chronic fatigue or illness, will find resources of all kinds directed at relaxation, a topic far more complex than one would imagine. This might start with a look into somatic therapy, the concern with nervous system health from the point of view of use. The underbelly of this movement has diversified quite a bit, but there is a backbone of medical and neuroscience support that has continued to validate and deepen the theory and practice of the related fields. Around the nuance and the admittedly useful exercises in the myriad approaches to somatic therapy, there is the notion that it all begins and ends with paying attention to sensations, and honoring them. The rabbit hole goes deep, and the surface is deceptively simple, which makes it even more confusing. However, somatic therapy is a bastion of natural health that we should look into. Some relevant names here include those of Peter Levine, Norman Doidge, and Stephen Porges.

The above are merely examples and simple guidelines. The idea is that each person will have to choose what they are most in need of developing or curing in themselves. Progression would mean that one of these practices becomes embedded, with sufficient knowledge to propel proper application, so that new areas of interest can be attended to efficiently. And while each person must follow an individual calling as to what is relevant and useful, there are a few obvious side quests that lead nowhere in particular and are a drain of time and resources. These include the obsession to learn many different languages without any concrete aim (are you going to write a book about it? Are you going to teach these languages? What are you going to DO with them?). Reading book after book on history, war, or magic and sorcery, amounts to the same, a kind of fetish. Equally useless is obsessive body building *for fun*, without a return flow in the form of money or usable status or health towards a *use*.

So many apparently respectable and useful things become obsessive distractions by the inability to be still and seriously consider what is *necessity* and what will actually facilitate an ascent. Most often, people stuck here have no access to guidance, or the value of guidance has been lost on them. It is as useless for a penniless man to be day-dreaming as it is for a well-off man to be working a day job "out of principle". Plan and act, acquire and use.

Mercurial and ethereal interests and their indulging are perfectly fine. But to those seeking dominion of their world, to break boundaries to their freedom and power, to enjoy life at a higher level, these must come within limits and context to your power and glory.

The Practice, not the Philosophy

Cynicism

One of the greater mental viruses of the modern age is the tendency for people to argue about principles without ever attempting the practice in whatever tradition or endeavor. Underneath it all lies cynicism, a cynicism encoded into the very fabric of modern thought and the defining feeling of the scientist age, the information age, of overload, of totalitarian thought control. However, it did not start here.

The precursor to the Enlightenment tyranny was Christianity, with its dogma of oppression and conquest, of universality. Christianity, of course, in its institutional and cultural sense, with its morality. Not because rules and guidelines are entirely undesirable, but because those chosen by Christianity were meant to stifle, to bind the individual. The Enlightenment preached the contrary but acted much the same. It was only an evolution of thought control. Each slave revolt needs a revision of the system of control. A new offering, a new allure, a new bait. Only Novalis caught on to the farce, and Goethe blocked his path for that.

So, today, the first question someone will ask you when invited or encouraged to do something is *why*. Even though, in theory, the scientific mind should only ask *how* and *why not*, because reason can only find out the means on the one hand, and disprove, on the other, but it cannot affirm the truth of a proposition regarding reality (by which we mean here, a *theory*) directly. People keep asking why, and supporting that why with prejudiced objections following a *but*. But everyone knows it doesn't work. But everyone knows it's bunk. But I don't think/know if it would work for me. But, but, but. That is, ideas before experience; often, laziness and apathy before a curious engagement with life, or at least the semblance of scientific interest.

Cynicism, in any case, is defeated easily. It is not a strong foundation for anything. If you hold a cynic attitude towards anything, you will have noticed that it takes energy to maintain that state. You need to remember *why* you are cynical. If you, in turn, asked *why not* be cynical, you would find plenty of reasons not to, and far superior to reasons for being cynical. The reasons for being cynical often amount to little more than resentment. Among the very concrete, down-to-earth reasons *why not* to be cynical are the fact that it causes constant stress and so forces your nervous system into an unsustainable stress (fight/flight/freeze) response that is, perhaps, the most common cause of premature aging, chronic fatigue, chronic illness, and much more.

Curiosity

ONE OF THE BEST WAYS to defeat cynicism is to engage in active, curious, playful exploration. Curiosity above all. We need curiosity. But curiosity of the experience. How does it feel, and what happens, when a certain experience takes place. We want to see things from the point of view of experience because experience is everything. No matter what you think or deduce or argue your mental models into later, it all comes from your individual experience of something. Reason comes later, and it is useful, it allows us to develop, to manipulate, so that we get what we want.

But reason without experience is empty. And to acquire experience, that is, to experience things (we want to use it as a verb as much as possible, because the word is a flux of events, not a landscape of abstractions), we must be curious. At least, if we want to experience things willingly and in a state of mind and conditions that we can control as much as possible (letting go of what we cannot). Otherwise, everything we experience will come from things that happen to us, that are imposed upon us.

The Use of Philosophy

PHILOSOPHY IS DEFINED as the love of knowledge. At least, in the mainstream. But this has been deformed, what with theology and the subsequent secular reaction to the infirmities of religious argument, and today it means some crude form of argumentation. Blame the interpreters of Socrates and Aristotle for this nonsense to begin with. Blame those who enthroned particularities of an ancient argument in context as the root and fountain of all philosophy. The calcification of ideas.

Love of knowledge, is it? If it is love of knowledge, then experience would be primary for the *philosopher*, and then reason, the power of argumentation, and logic, its tool, would be used to organize, to prod, to move forward and *experience* yet again, with more clarity. Philosophy cannot be an end. Experience must always be the end, because experience is life, experience is all we have, every moment, every single conscious moment. Philosophy in the favor of ideologies or religions is an empty exercise; it has to do with the building of vast edifices of abstractions which have nothing to do with *experience* (the only source of *realness*).

But, only experience is real.

All else is a model, a road map. Experience is the territory. Sure, Kant and physics tell us that what we perceive is only a fraction of the "real". But what of it? All this tells us is that we must deepen experience, because there is always more to discover, or that we can further course correct and perceive things more clearly, in more detail, or from a different angle. In any case, philosophy, on the contrary, can sometimes be but a map. And the map—is not the territory.

In all cases, the philosophy must serve the experience, and so should the science, the systematic application of reason. This is how we adhere to reality, by upholding the primacy of individual experience which is then compared, shared, validated or examined in comparison to that of others. Whether a reported experience fits a model or a theory should not be the disqualifying point, instead, it should go on file for possible evidence that disqualifies the theory. Once enough reported experiences from upstanding, credible individuals are turned in have accumulated, the notion should be validated that something *real* is happening for which the model cannot account. Back to the drawing board.

Why NOT Lucid Dreaming and Astral Projection?

Objections

"What's the point?" What's the point of anything? Lucid Dreaming and Astral Projection seem like insanely fun things to do, vastly superior to video games or digital virtual realities. They are also, reportedly, ways to get information quickly and at a distance. Yes, this is disputed even by people who are proficient in both, but the mere possibility of all of these things is stimulating to many people.

"But it takes so much time and effort." That depends. And besides, anything worth doing, and that you are going to derive great dividends from, is likely to take time and effort. This objection will only deter the kind of person who will not work for anything in their life for more than two seconds.

"Why would I *believe* these things are even real." Well, for one, Lucid Dreaming has been proven in a laboratory setting and is considered a factual experience since at least the late 70s. In the case of the Out-of-Body Experience (aka Astral Projection), it has been reported for thousands of years by scores of people. Just in the last one hundred and fifty years there have been compilations of these experiences put together by living credible people, gathering such accounts from other living credible people. You could look into the work of Robert Crookall for these references.

Implications

LUCID DREAMING AND Astral Projections are frameworks for disembodied experiences. In essence all dreaming is an Out-of-Body Experience (OBE) because you are not acting in an environment with your physical body. This is why Michael Raduga has opted for calling all conscious disembodied states *the phase*. The only downside to Raduga's approach, and it is an understandable downside, is that his research subscribes to the materialist notion. It appears that he believes that all experience and consciousness arises from the brain, or the nervous system, at any rate.

Wider implications, unfettered by materialist assumptions, should be obvious. We are not just conventionally considered material bodies, and our consciousness can exist separate from the body. Now, while many people at this point go wild with assumptions, this does not prove immortality not even the fact that we can exist without the body. Unfortunately many smart people jump wagon here and go full spiritualist in one go.

While there are indications that some people's consciousness have survived bodily death, we do not know if this is an immortality situation, or of it is just a matter of gradually fading into oblivion. The only thing Lucid Dreaming proves is that we can consciously take control of our dreams. The only thing OBEs prove is that we can experience a facet of consciousness in a state that appears to us, for all practical purposes, to take place outside of the body.

Lucid Dreaming is proven "objectively", that is validated even for people who report never having had this experience. Astral Projection is only validated between people who have had this experience.

From the practical point of view, of attaining any of these experiences, Raduga's perspective is useful. Instead of thinking you must transcend into another plane, you simply acknowledge the fact that every night you dream, and every time you dream you have the possibility of becoming aware that you are dreaming, i.e. to become lucid. In that state, you have the chance of going into a full-blown astral projection. According to Raduga, the difference between the dream, the lucid dream and the astral projection is a matter of degree. The Phase, as he calls it, is this brain-produced experience. Raduga is very wise in approaching the experience this way, purposefully avoiding any philosophical discussions, ducking arguments, tying the very mystical experience of astral projection to an already objectively proven phenomenon in lucid dreaming. This way, he becomes eligible for public funding, and is more accessible for mainstream consideration.

For the individual practitioner, taking what works from Raduga and then discovering how these alternate realities work is the most productive. The idea that it is all connected, for one, can facilitate success. But it is the implication which we must manage. The implications must remain open-ended until experience connects certain dots. And even then, conclusions must never supersede experience.

Remote Viewing for Stabilizing the Artist's State of Flow

The idea of remote viewing as a martial art was brought to our attention by Joseph McMoneagle as he draws parallels between the remote viewing need to reach a level of mental stability and openness akin to that found in Zen practice and the spirit of Japanese martial arts. While in the first chapter of his book, *Remote Viewing Secrets: A Handbook*, MacMoneagle proceeds to install subliminal linguistic directives into the reader for the purpose of setting mental safeguards preventing rogue behavior as much as possible, he also communicates useful pointers for the practice of remote viewing which could have an application to progress and mastery of any activity. Ideas such as not aiming for perfection but for the mind-quieted state of flow that brings through a constant stream of perceptions, have a somewhat similar echo in the rules for learning that Feldenkrais developed as a consequence of his Judo training.

One of the most salient features of remote viewing is that you should put down exactly what you perceive and nothing—we repeat—*nothing* else. The state of mind required is that of total presence, something we experience when in a duel, a physical altercation, whether in tournament or outside, but also during the act of sexual intercourse—if properly approached. These acts consume our minds entirely, and there is a magic released therein that comes from the fact that we are able to engross ourselves so deeply and with all our senses that we exist nowhere else at any other point in time. At least, that is how it feels. It is a state of flow, or what some would rather term *the zone*.

This state is also sought by artists and scientists alike. A state in which ideas, schemata, pictures, all come in completed form, all outside the step-wise, cumbersome ways of reason. In other words, the highway of inspiration. Conventionally, the highest form of artists know that when inspiration hits, they must take advantage of this moment. So do scientists. The cleverest among them will have developed an "ear", so to speak, of what state of mind personally brings about such state of flow, such inspiration that is an openness to intuition, to messages in completed form, perhaps even to a kind of Platonic world of forms extant somewhere beyond the veil.

Remote viewing training aims at making the practitioner able to enter this state at will, on demand. The protocols aimed at directing consciousness to take advantage of this state do so with the specific and explicit aim of gathering technical sensory information. Nevertheless, it is admitted by military professionals such as Ed Dames that the controlled remote viewing protocol can be used to obtain more speculative type of answers concerning decisions or the existence of a certain target object. This tells us there could also be a way of adapting controlled remote viewing protocols to facilitate artistic flow.

Where does imagination enter, you might ask. Herein lies the confusion, while there is much imagination in art, be it literature, music, sculpture, poetry, or anything else, all of the best artists, as well as the best appreciators of art, will concur that the best art does not come from mere imagination. Its is admitted among whispers that the greatest art comes from "elsewhere", behind the seat of the mind, from a greater awareness, a greater consciousness of which the regular individual mind is but a drop, a tendril among trillions.

The essential elements of the remote viewing protocol, abstracted in order to produce a working model applicable to the artistic process, are three. The first is veiling or avoiding attempts to prematurely define the final result as much as possible. The second is being able to rhythmically record flash-impressions coming as pulses into awareness before the process of imaginative construction gets started. The third is having a framework of vessels into which the aforementioned impressions will be recorded; that is, a systematic way of giving form to the energy, perhaps in the form of archetypes.

In literature in particular, many are the character and plot building frameworks that seek to give would-be writers a guide to clear expositions. Oftentimes, these result in weak, stale products which, even if successful, are recognized as artistic failures and empty caricatures but more sensitive demanding personalities. The problem, it would seem, is that the workers of literature more prone to using prepared character and plot frameworks are not the kind that connect well with higher artistic principles. On the other hand, more accomplished, sensitive artists, readily see in frameworks a tying of their hands, a limiting of their creativity. The latter confuse creativity with inspiration, the real source of breakthrough original works of art. Not even Heidegger can convince us otherwise. The ground of being demands to be listened to, while all the noise around, all the appearing, and the will to appear, interrupts communication, distorts the message.

If all the strangeness and intensity of the spirit of Stravinsky's Rite of Spring could be funneled into potent vessels with shapes like those dreamed up by Giger, and mounted on a progressive sequence of scenes each commanding more interest and tension than the one before, and yet each a standalone aesthetic pleasure, you would have a magnetic work of towering genius.

But to make a system and method of training that allows the artist to summon such forces to his aid, a conscious adherence to protocol, and at the same time a relinquishing of personal control, would have to occur. The creation of an unusual system of vessels arranged for plot and depth, defined in their contours but not their total flavor, in their order and relations, but not their actions. And then a wild recording of chaos, punctuated by pauses to halt and divert the plot-building impulses of the mind; a record of these chaotic outbursts, preferably in states violent and sensual, would be summoned up by quick prompts to be "probed into" without thinking and followed up by spasmodic event-recording.

The possibilities are many, the road more demanding than before, yet the end also more promising for the adventurous artist.

Journal—Intensely

Journal your daily events, the stages of your life, your dreams, what did not happen but could have happened, summon the ghosts of the past and the future, visit alternate timelines, gain wisdom from the multiverse. This, and much more, is why you should journal—*intensely*.

The Intense Journal Method was created by the Jewish psychiatrist Ira Progoff. It stems from Jungian notions, principally, that there exist, somewhere in consciousness, forms called archetypes, living forms representing ideas and concepts, and with which one can interact as one would with a sentient being. The approach would perfectly blend in within a therapeutic setting, while it would not be alien to the occult altogether.

Progoff's main idea is that one journal would contain different section in which you would attend to different levels and perspectives of your mind, understanding by putting it all together into one work that your experience is all united with yourself as a nexus. On different sections of the journal you would be exploring hard facts without embellishments, while on others you would explore events that never happened but could have.

Recording dreams, something that is also included in the Intense Journal Method, has been singled out as the most straightforward and useful way for beginners to start lucid dreaming. Although this does not seem to have been Progoff's main motivation for including a dream log in the method, it is a welcome added benefit. Lucidity tends not to arrive by accident. Independently of whether it comes through the act of logging your dream experiences, getting into the habit of questioning whether you are in a dream throughout the day, or looking at your hands periodically (yes, this actually works), the lucid experience comes from a conscious decision to enhance awareness of direct experience. What direct experience means here is detailed attention to sensory input while acting, to the exclusion of building constructs, getting carried away by emotions or lost in thoughts. It is an exercise that can be practiced while awake, making it a habit for yourself to do this at all time. If the effort is serious, this will quickly result in a spillover into your dreaming experience.

Journaling will also help you revise your daily habits. Humans have a legendary ability to tell themselves stories about what they are doing, what they want, and where they want to go. One of the things that will happen when you start logging your days is that leaks and habits that do not match your *ideas* of what you are doing with your life are quickly exposed. The divergence between what you believe you desire and the actions you are taking on the daily appear now as a very noticeable rift. You can then either look away and try to ignore it or you revise that relationship. That is, it is not always a matter of correcting the course of your actions to meet your stated desires. Very often, what is really happening is that what you tell yourself you want comes from the outside, from constructs, or from an overactive imagination, or a logical mind bouncing down a staircase of deductive possibilities.

The revising of a life, defining the important milestones along it, and revisiting the crucial feelings and possibilities that existed from one era to another, has been a process that psychologists and psychiatrists of different stripes have acknowledged as useful and as usually having a great impact. The Intensive Journal Method also has a space for doing so. Besides the more obvious excavation of old problematic feelings that were in the past bottled up and started causing problems, we can see how revising the distant past ties in with the daily log. Your actions and decisions are laid out before you so that you start to gain clarity of why you are where you are, and clues arise as to why there has been any confusion to begin with.

Moreover, as the different logs in the journal start to fill out, and more thought experiments and Jungian explorations start to take place, the instructions for the Intensive Journal will start to guide you into making connections from one area of the journal into another. When that happens, you will start to weave a braid with the levels of consciousness and areas of life experience, so that the boundaries between these which were initially of much use in pin-pointing aspects of an experience, become blurred, and the perception of life starts to arise as the interlinked mass of events and processes that it is. At this point, it is not just that one becomes aware of the river and the different elements in it, nor that one allows the flow to take precedence, but a certain mastery of several currents starts to become possible. This can only be discovered individually. The present is an invitation.

Walking the Tightrope

A false dichotomy

Wellness and devotion, self-care and self-discipline, accomplishment and satisfaction; we are told we must choose between these, that one ingrains us here on earth, and on the walls of the ethereal halls of the gods, while the other is a waste of our existence by way of indulgence. In occult parlance, the proposition that discipline defined by the divine is the only way, and that individual indulgence is inadequate, constitutes the beginning of the bifurcation of the path of esoteric attainment into the Left and Right Hand paths. The interested reader can look further into the abundant extant literature on this division.

When we look closely at this matter, without prejudice or partisanship, we can understand that both sides have a point. On the one hand, there are habits and lifestyles that lead to self-destruction, to blindness, and to constant suffering. On the other, it would not make sense to say no to the pleasures of existence for the sake of an invisible, a promised, salvation in a future or a reality we cannot even grasp.

From there, more becomes obvious. First, that there must exist a middle path neither to one extreme nor the other. Second, that this middle path should address and satisfy the concerns the more it is perfected. Beyond the immediately evident, divergences in opinions and in preference highlight the need for each person's path to be tailored to themselves as a unique vector mapped across multiple higher dimensions. How and what these are can be best left to individual exploration and an eventual convergence of related experience.

Absolute self-interest

FROM OUR POINT OF VIEW, the perfected path that unites the proper, the constructive, the ennobling, with the enjoyment of pleasure, the satisfaction of thirst for knowledge and experience, lies in absolute self-interest. Note that we do not mean selfishness or egoism in the conventional uses of these words. The words hide more than it seems, and they point to a demanding process whereby self-satisfaction leads not to careless indulgence but to a bringing about of the person's deepest desires.

We humans have been referred to as matrices. There is the greater matrix within which we all interact, and within which also greater symbols and possibilities float and resonate with or repel each other. But the individual matrix of the human encasing has to do with whatever you bring as a conscious observer, the body into which you were set (the ancients would have thought this determines *destiny* and *fate*, depending on calibration), and the degree of awareness (i.e. the degree to which you are awake and aware that you are an observer of experience at the very core).

In following this model of the interrelations between elements of reality being one large matrix comprised of an ocean and hierarchy of matrices within matrices, outside influences, the trends, the important symbols that affect and influence our lives, lie somewhere close to us, at least in magnitude and significance. So, it becomes evident that not all that you desire, not all that you think and feel, belongs necessarily to you. Thoughts and feelings are signals. They are not good or bad, and they may have different sources. It is no wonder why the central practice of meditation, and to some extent prayer, have to do with increasing awareness and a connection to existence while allowing these signals to pass by unheeded. As we progress our ability to differentiate the source of the signals improves. A distinct path to a deeper source within and beyond ourselves becomes clearer.

Absolute self-interest, our proposed concept, leads to a doubling down, a concentrating, in the awareness of the boundaries of the individual, the extent of their interests in terms of mental magnetism (a term here loosely used, without conscious relation to the New Thought movement), and the development of what the individual is geared to by virtue of the body and time given to them.

The first filter: Know thyself

TO KNOW THYSELF IS a very old adage. A story is told that you can take the time to look into. Philosophical discussions around it abound. The core of the matter is that to arrive at self-knowledge sounds simple, because the work is straightforward, but it is nevertheless hard. You may be reminded that you know what you must do, but you also realize it is not easy to do. That is not to say that the actions you are called to take are necessarily hard, but rather the decision to willingly endure the friction, to go against the inertia of your past actions, and including the possible social fallout and rejection or setting aside of mores and morals you had till then upheld as true.

Practitioners of Tao and Zen are well-aware of the dictum, *sleep when tired, eat when hungry*. Not a state, but a process. Now, how does this tie in with knowing oneself? Let's take a closer look.

Religious movements will seek refuge in prophets, in leaders who *we must trust* are in contact with the divine. All while acknowledging that God, the divine, the greater or deeper Self, however one wants to approach the phenomenon, exist in constant, permanent, connection with each of us. All that keeps you from that direct connection and instead paying attention to someone else about what you should or should not do is fear, and the lack of dedication that can lead you to the establishment and strengthening of that direct link to the point where no intermediaries are necessary.

It is very possible that the deceptively simple approach of the Oriental tradition contained within the phrase *sleep when tired, eat when hungry* contains the basic practice to *follow your impulse* in the deepest sense. To learn to really listen to the pains and aches, the needs, the joys, and warnings, and so on, that come through with your body. Whatever we are, ultimately, irrespective of modes presented to us by one or other tradition, the fact of the matter is that we process all incoming signals in the form of sensations, either directly in the body or similar translations into feelings and intuitions in the nervous system. Whether the perception of these signals originate in the physical body or elsewhere is beside the point. The point is to listen closely, and eventually achieve a more nuanced differentiation of their nature and origin.

The art of distinguishing the different impulses and learning to *choose for oneself* could fill tomes (a work that we might undertake, given time, but the time is too early for a work of such metaphysical magnitude), yet the practice consists almost solely of paying attention and remaining aware of what goes on. Pleasure and pain will come and go, and what we feel most compelled to choose constitutes desire. The choice that comes from the unwavering place no matter the mood nor preference of the day qualifies as an authentic desire. We say this to distinguish desire from caprice. Desire arises from magnetism, and when one speaks or writes too much about it, the text rapidly devolves into vagaries, into a pastiche of sophistries. It is therefore imperative that the interested party make of the affair a practice, a habit, and that he incorporates it into daily life, so that from the notion's seed a stem and leaves grow green, and, finally, that a flower blossom therefrom.

The second filter: Do what works

DESIRE (DISCOVERED, cultivated, allowed to grow) serves as a compass. We might descend too deep into speculation if unguarded, but let us venture to say that if there are indeed physical and nonphysical aspects to us, desire might come from the physical matrix and also from some ulterior place, connected to a preternatural origin. Why even go into this territory unaided by scores of theological artillery or some kind of authority to back it up? Firstly, and aside from the reason that is pertinent here, to the authentically thinking person, argument and authority matter very little. A satanist would even say they matter less than nothing. Secondly, a careful self-examination can very easily yield plausible explanations as to why one holds one desire or another. Quite often, asking oneself out loud or writing the question down with the intent of getting an answer is enough to trigger a first response. To keep digging, one keeps asking, intelligently, why, for what purpose, and so on, and comparing the answers that come to mind with the feelings that arise in parallel. Self-honesty will reveal that the answers have been known all along. Certain things are liked, indulged in, sought, simply because friends, environment, or perhaps even the alignment of the stars (ask Ptolemy) guided us there. If we stop and *observe* and allow the sensations that come with the perception of said influences move through us, as one would with pain and emotion (ask Shinzen Young), they are washed away, by the force and current of the same waves that brought them to our doorstep. Then there remains the thinnest of threads, the yearnings which have no visible link to your living experiences, nor to the circumstances of your upbringings. The mark upon these will be twofold. First will be the aforementioned lack of a conscious link to anything palpable in your mortal life. Second will be the consistency inherent in them, the sense of permanency, revealed by the fact that as you hold still, they, too, shall hold still *with you*.

    What will work in the long run for the individual without doing violence to the Self (and to the body), will likely have something to do with these desires with preternatural links. But what will work also has two aspects. The first is, as mentioned, determined by the motivating desire's relation to the Self, the Lord, the Observer. The second concerns method and circumstance to implement the road of action once the aim has been determined. This is the other side of the coin. With one hand you reach deep into yourself and you let the world move around. With the other, you feel out the terrain, for the terrain is all-important here, and the route taken must adapt to it. The search for, the building of, the seeking of a desired state, would be best served, for your own sake, by the most efficient means.

Doing what works, as described above, has levels to it, and levels that are deeply personal, defined by individuality. How they are attended to, organized, promoted or demoted, can only be discovered through the first step, knowing yourself. The process might not end, but it does not mean that further and further stability and strength are not gained. They are, if one succeeds, which is a matter of putting in the work. The greatest distractions to realizing the core work are caprices and a false sense of belonging to a greater whole wherein individuality is lost, for the sake of a dream given, curated, and dictated for a purpose alien to yourself. So, choose, or a choice will be made for you. And then, again, and so on.

Doing what works works along an axis sustained by *what works for you* and *what works for the environment*. You cannot disregard either of them and expect for things to go smoothly. Things will go the smoothest when you *pay attention* and develop *acuity*, the capacity to perceive states and changes in states, and the talent to adapt to them, switching gears until a variation of approach clicks.

Some things are, nevertheless, unavoidable and are part of the nature of reality. The work must be put it. It does not mean it needs to be hard. Difficulty as a measure of the worthiness or value of an effort is a red herring. But to learn, to allow for adaptations in neurology and other physiology to take place, repetition, reinforcement and consistency in general must be in place. So much, we all know.

The only measure of worthiness, at the end of the day, remains in the question: *Does It Work?*

All else is hubris.

"It don't matter what you believe"

Once direct experiencing of your senses becomes primary, it becomes quite clear that thoughts and emotions are circumstantial. Beliefs and convictions fall by the wayside. The focus upon what is happening around you, what your eyes perceive, your ears hear, and the relationships between input and output become clearer and clearer, the models political, ideological, religious, cosmological, and so on, for the world, that a person might have are revealed as spurious, as irrelevant.

To the average person walking in the street, whether the Earth is flat, round, spherical, cubic, pyramidal or tetrahedral, has no relevance at all. What matters to you as you walk out the door, look up at the sky, see the curvature of the dome above, enjoy the play of colors in the firmament with the sun setting into the distance, many miles away into the horizon, is that you are experiencing these things, as you see them, this very moment. The models for the shape of the planet do not change the world around you, just as the different psychological models for human mind do not change your experience as a person after you have learned to focus on direct observation.

Abraham Maslow came up with the pyramid of needs. Is it accurate? Where did he get this? How did he gather this data? There is common sense in the thing, but is it universal? Does it apply in every case? More importantly, would you forget to be hungry, to want a mate, to seek out respect and status, if you had never seen Maslow's model of human needs painted on a screen or a book? It is doubtful.

The facts and forces will accumulate, and reality will make you notice it exists. It will do so in no uncertain terms. Tread carefully, we must. That does not mean reality does not evolve, that the rules do not change. Nor that the past may not change. Large scale random number generator experiments in the area of parapsychology have yielded results that indicate that collective willpower can bend probabilistic expectations towards the unlikely. And yet, there is a persistence, a loyalty to what has actually happened, that no mass deception campaign can succeed in changing the past into a fairy tale unless most of the people who knew it to be false are killed off.

What you believe, will only add layers to what you can see, hear and touch. Sometimes, these things are useful. Most of the time, they lead you into patterns of thoughts designed to direct you in accordance with a greater will. So, the question we have to ask ourselves remains, master or slave. *What will ye?*

Where beliefs matter

Belief matters as a trigger for action. Belief, for the savvy practitioner, should never be confused with reality. It should be, nevertheless, included as a tool among many. The problem of the majority is to be consumed by belief, duped by belief. Belief constructs a system of assumptions, honing your mind into certain lines of thought and so of possible action. Belief will also foster certain desires to the exclusion of others. It acts as a filter between possible events surrounding you and the experiences that become plausible for you.

We do not mean here to say that mere superficial belief is going to change reality. A superficial belief is usually the will to disbelieve something else; that is, the person *trying* to belief, or pretending to believe something is only running away from something else. The art of believing and disbelieving at will requires a very clear cognizance of the nature of belief in relation to reality.

The application of belief for its best effect, however, can be a bit tricky. Too much of it and it can cloud your judgment, lead you astray, and leave you in a fairyland of your own making. That is precisely the case with most people that we could say fall in the mind-controlled category. They share an illusion, or a delusion, and they are completely unaware of it. But the best use of belief is the conscious use of an illusion that enhances focus, that filters out the unnecessary, and makes things *click* for us. Most important here is also that last bit: *for us*.

Perform Trials, then Confirm or Reject

INSTEAD OF BELIEF (or its corresponding opposite force, *disbelief*), we want to approach our subject and our actions with as clean a mind as possible, using our power to reason in the most scientific way possible, rather than to spin stories that can then be layered over what is happening.

While belief has its uses, if we are always aware that we are simply putting on a suit when using it, we are really just adhering to a model rather than developing a belief (or a "blind belief", as people commonly say). To use this terminology is more clear. We do not believe in things, we simply use a model that so far works well for our purposes. If the model yields results, then we have a functional tool. Otherwise, it is not the model we need.

Trusting Sensations

Poetry, abstract and tangible

One of the lessons W.B. Yeats imparted to Ezra Pound was that abstractions muddied communication, they introduced barriers to communication. Reportedly, the older poet told the younger one to look through his poems and see how many abstractions he could find. And it seems he found many such abstractions in his text, to his own surprise. As he moved forward, Pound sought to transform his expression into more something more graspable, with objects and motions at the very center of his work.

While Pound later stirred into a mystic obscurantism and rhythmic experimentation, it is quite obvious that the dictum of avoiding abstraction was preserved. Understand or not, we can recognize the symbols, the agents, the scenes, and the actions depicted line after line in his poetry. And even when we do not recognize a name or title, nor even the context, we know that what stands before us is a symbol, a person, or an agent—a personality, at any rate.

When we pay attention to what happens inside ourselves as we shift a conversation from descriptive actions to abstractions, we will become aware of a sort of disconnection, as if we are no longer, not entirely, *here*. The eyes become glazed, they stare nowhere. The typical look of the mystic or the dreamer is that of someone who has left the present, shared reality. The disconnection occurs with the body itself and in great part with other people around them. This type of person is not misunderstood or sundered socially because they or their ideas are strange or special, in the sense of them being hard to come by. They are simply harder to understand for most people because of how they are expressed. If one cared to pay attention, the highest philosophical ideas, if they make any sense at all, can be found all over the artistic production of the human mind. More importantly, you will come across these ideas in the events of daily life.

Plato and the World of Forms

LET US CONSIDER FOR a moment that abstraction comes as a mistrust of the senses. We will not argue that abstraction begun with Christianity, for we can find abstract thought before. Now, some have said point blank that abstracting itself lead to the downfall of humanity, much like Gibbon wrote Christianity had been the downfall of the Roman Empire. Many agreed with him. We also know that Christians and Muslims praise Aristotle and Plato, coming very close to naming them *honorary* members of their religions. What these two shared with the aforementioned religions was that impulse to abstraction.

May we come in Plato's defense and point out that his depictions of discussions of abstractions were couched in dialogues, and that said dialogues in the mouth of Socrates and his differing companions tended to resort to concrete examples. Thus, happiness was never left as an abstraction, but was always brought down to earth. We can, in fact, see Socrates as the hero who always makes concrete the abstract. Plato makes sure we are always coming back to particulars, to actions. Even as there is a *world of forms* above ours, for which his ideas are mainly known, it is not so much the imaginary *world of abstractions* of modern scholarship, as it is, possibly, something more akin to the *astral world* of modern occultism.

The impulse to act, the signal to respond, neuroscience experiments have shown, comes before the conscious mind is aware of that the action is taking place. The reasoning mind organizes, makes plans, abstracts and feeds this back. It rationalizes decisions. The act itself, the action, comes from something either *behind* it or *above* it.

Consciously, we become aware of what we sense, in the actions that are taking place, in the inputs we receive from the outside, and in the impulses that come deep from within us. And so it would appear that to know and control more, we must be very careful with abstraction and rationalization. As with other mental constructs, they can be useful tools and allies, as well as terrible traps and traitors.

Ownership and Value, An Example of the Traps of Abstraction

ABSTRACTIONS CAN BE helpful in organizing and moving things around inside our heads, but if we are seeking to extend our capacity in the world, to do, to experience, and so on, they cannot supersede our sensations. Very often, abstractions are used to hoodwink, to divert, and they are prominently recognized as part of the arsenal of sorcery (*this is not a poetic exaggeration or embellishment*). While we do not endorse ideologies of any kind, we do understand that our society has embraced abstract concepts to the point where the useful verges on abusive.

One such abstract concept, ownership, was useful as long as it concerned the *respect* afforded an individual as to his claim to be the main user of an object. It is entirely based on an invented rule so that there can be an understanding between two individuals. In truth, ownership does not exist. Thinking it does is being deluded. Such delusion is what lies at the root of many individuals feeling surprised, or even "appalled", when people with greater power and absolutely no respect for them see it fit to transgress the boundaries of said ownership. Your things may be destroyed, taken away, and so on, and short of retribution by way of the law or your own hands, there is no stopping it. The concept of ownership will not stop it.

The *agreement* of ownership, as any other social abstraction, can only exist as a *compromise* between individuals. It is a compromise towards peace. If no such peace is desired, and if no respect is forthcoming, you can be sure abstractions will not come to your aid.

The delusion of ownership, to continue with this particular example, allows for even more covert means of subversion. Imagine you are told that, in exchange for your work and effort you will be given tokens, or "credits". Imagine then, that these tokens or credits do not have a fixed value, but that they fluctuate. In fact, as a general rule, they will automatically and indefinitely become less and less valuable as time goes by. This, of course, will not happen on its own. The value that you have acquired did not just disappear. The effect of your actions did not simply fizzle out. Energy does not disappear. The value and recompense of your actions continues moving in effect, along and across people and processes. You, however, will only receive a one-time, depreciating token, the value of which is a caprice, in exchange for the potentially infinite benefit you give to others. The tokens are a useful con, but a con nonetheless. The abstraction at the root of the great fraud is the concept of *value*.

The argument here is not a Marxist one. Marx's single pony trick revolves around "correctly" calculating value and arguing in favor of a more "just" system. What we are pointing out here, in contrast, is that the ground upon which all such arguments exist is an artifice.

The Power in the Senses

REMOTE VIEWING IN PARTICULAR was designed with the explicit purpose of eliminating the distracting effects of abstraction, rationalization and identification from the process of direct perception. The whole purpose of the systematic protocols of remote viewing have to do with getting rid of the deductions and associations, of the wistful creativity, and to simply *perceive what is*.

The degree to which importance is laid on this aspect is so great that in the old days, reportedly, remote viewers in training were suggested to study and practice the drawing exercises in Betty Edward's book *Drawing on the Right Side of the Brain*. Said exercises emphasize creating in oneself the habit of only capturing the information that is brought to our eyes by the light, and nothing else. Usually, we pass over things, identifying and categorizing them. We see a lamp or a chair, and what we tend to consciously remember and picture is an archetypal lamp or chair. What we see, however is an arrangement of shadows upon a screen of light that comes to the retina of the eye. We *touch the world* with our eyes.

Entering the *phase*, as Michael Raduga calls lucid dreaming and the out-of-body experience, is all about a *deepening of physical sensations*. This flies in the face of most "astral" rhetoric of the New Age and "occult" variety. Raduga, however, a single-minded beast of tremendous willpower turned educator and scientist, cares only for effective procedures divested of veiling rhetoric.

Phasing procedures, the protocols taught by Michael Raduga, hitherto known as "awakening in dreams", "projecting into the astral", "going into a hypnagogic state of mind", and so on, consist from beginning to end in utilizing different techniques that bring to increasing focus and activation the function of one or another physical sense while remaining physically still. Imagining, visualizing, is only used as a secondary psychic driving technique, so as to predispose the mind towards a definite result. All is included for merely functional uses directed at producing said result. Nevertheless, at the forefront of all is to sink into the sensations, to test sensations, to *enhance* sensations, to the point you can hear, touch, smell, move, and so on more and more independently of the situation or condition in which the physical body is.

Modern Art and Abstraction

THE SIGNATURE OF ALL modern art is its tendency to abstract, to go from actuals to conceptuals, to subvert perception of aesthetic through argument, to impose the mind upon the senses, and then to claim that such inversion is the authentic, the natural. The argument can also take the form of an entire dismissal of the natural. They do so by claiming that the idea of something being natural or unnatural is entirely conceptual. Because in effect, this is true, here is where a muddying of the waters of the mind takes place.

We exist as total beings with sets of faculties, abilities, and so on, that allow us to sense the world, organize it, distinguish patterns. Our internal chemistry and electric patterns react, redefining the shape of texture and organ, bone and muscle, rallying the thunderstorm roaring in the brain into battles. The real is the whole of this apparent chaos (which it is not). We exist as individuals because there is pattern, because personality and individuality arise, and because we sense, as a species and then as a subset of that, as individuals.

The great deception, the great enslavement, consists in this: making us forget about the sensations, forget about the world, forget about the internal movements of the body, and their extensions, as primary. Instead, we are given images, longings outside of ourselves. This is not an argument against ego or desire. On the contrary, the root and fountain of these lies within, through the senses.

Just Enough

One of the traps of being oriented towards self-education and of having great intellectual curiosity for things is to get bogged down in a swamp of theory and accounts for far longer than is necessary. While each new endeavor requires a manner of guidance, the basic foundational skills of almost any discipline, need only a straightforward instruction. The rest is consistent practice.

There is something else to know, another book to read, another author to consult, a different way of doing things. You could go on indefinitely, discovering new patterns and paradigms. Potentially, there are as many ways of projecting as conscious beings in the world, in addition to the permutations introduced by collaboration and interaction, and the variations thereof. But we, as individuals, can either remain the spectators of the show, or we can become participants. Furthermore, the degree to which we become the sole captains and decision makers of our every action and stylistic choice, as well as knowers of our desires, is the degree to which we become the main actors within our individual perceptions.

What we are advocating is cutting, simply cutting. The idea, as received here, comes from Miyamoto Musashi, the famous Japanese duelist. Infamous on the arena, the warrior emphasized practicality and trusting the senses. He argued for a state of emptiness. While we are not experts in Eastern philosophy, we reserve the right to expound our interpretations of these words through our experience through life, through effort. Void, in its most functional aspect, has simply to do to stop fantasizing and overelaborating, over-extending. Some would say that you "become one" with your surroundings. Others, closer to home, would say you are "extending your senses". As a rule, we would rather say you are *paying attention* to what is going on. And this, to an uncommonly experienced degree that allows you to move and react with the ever-changing chain of cause and effect, even before it unfolds.

The point of consumption, if one is to take control of one's world, is to enable, to feed, to grow stronger, to assimilate, to become more lethal, to take more heads, shrinking them and having the spirits within them serve us. Each person shall take these words as they will, in accordance with their predisposition and prejudice, or, hopefully, lack thereof.

Hundreds if not thousands of fatalists and decadents can argue. For it is their right to indulge for no reason at all. Their birthright to wallow in apathy and decide it is not for them to accept the animal inside, but only feed it palliatives to dampen the pain of the hungry wound. They say they indulge the wound, befriend the beast, and you will forgive them for they know not what they say, and certainly not what they do.

But you, what will you do?

Hereby do we incite all in our train, or within sight of it, to indulge in creation, referencing just enough, consuming to strengthen, and to produce non-stop. Journals, drawings, manifestos, methods, businesses, whatever it is. For they are a manifestation of your power and glory. Whoever tries to convince us that all is lost, that we can do nothing, because we are nothing, has something to gain from our consumption of their words, their products, and in some way or other, you become food for them. We reject such a path. We take just enough for our benefit, to enhance our knowledge, and so our power. And we rise.

World Domination

Push everything away, and allow your desire alone to remain. This is the road we have increasingly taken on our journey of accomplishment. As far as we can see, it works for everything. It is also a tricky thing.

When you follow every whim, chances are you are being diverted into giving away your time, money, energy, and so on, to something that gives you nothing back, or just a temporary respite from your suffering. You suffer because you want more life, more power, more choice, more of your desires laid on your lap.

When we underline remote viewing and the out-of-body experience as expedient roads to a form of power over your life, we did so under the pretense of these things opening unknown doors, doors that reveal more of what you want and give you more choices, more possibilities. We also know that some will resonate with the prospect and the method, and others will not. This is as expected and is for the best, for it is in line with following desire. You should do this and all other things because it is what you desire, one way or another.

Follow this line of thinking, examine the why of your every decision, and you will find hidden desires under things you consciously reject or detest about your life. The slave loves being a slave, the subdued is addicted to hating and desires to be told what to do and given sustenance in the mouth.

Subliminal Self-Subversion

ANTON LAVEY, IN ONE of his many essays, later collected shortly before or after his death, argued in favor of acquiring total control of subliminal influence over oneself. A tantalizing proposition, the precise method he gave was to create all sensory inputs you would customarily consume. These included all the forms of art in which you would indulge, as well as an extreme personalization of your living surroundings. Furthermore, LaVey suggested we record psychic driving tapes (read as self-hypnosis), "self-help" tapes, and so on, voodoo-like dolls and other paraphernalia extremely customized to your desires and worldly designs.

We need not operate exactly as the founder of the Church of Satan intended. His suggestion is, in fact, to act in whatever matter most pleases you and expresses your personality.

Now, imagine being free enough, in mind and intention, to create the music you would rather listen, write the novels and research you would see carried out, living in a house where every corner, symbol displayed, and so on, has a meaning and an effect that is in line with your aim, either through pleasure or displeasure (for both can be harnessed to your benefit).

Increasingly, the scenario becomes akin to the ill-named Chaos Magick of Peter J. Carroll et al. As the artist deepens in his personalization of the total experience of life under self-influence, even the symbols he uses, the divinities he worships, arise from a cosmos entirely of his own making. A blind Ouroboros, self-consuming and self-directed. It is said that somehow, sometime, if the individual survives the onslaught brought about by their own deluge, the cyclonic power of the process starts to spill over into the worlds (perception-domains) of other conscious entities (including that of other humans).

Lawlessness and the Outlaw

RIDING THE INCESSANT waves of the Will, clashing rhythmically and cyclically against the rocky coastline of our physical body, we discover the inner life of the outlaw. The only law turns out to be the attainment of our desires, their full-fledged and unrestrained indulgence. The only measure of worthiness and success is how much both the road and the never-ending process please us. The moment they cease to do so, you have gone wrong.

Think not in terms of pigeonholed philosophical categories. Think in terms of functions, of remaking and retaking mechanistic contraptions to make something of your own. We do not advocate a motley approach, wherein you end up with a patchwork of mismatched symbols and semi-truths. What we mean is that where you find truth that *serves your budding desire*, take it. Take it as it suits you, take it out of context, as long as it works in your context. Make it yours. For the outlaw, it is their own law that matters alone.

Hence the bare-bones methods and approaches suggested by us. That they may serve all the highly individual readers approaching our publications. Because we do not preach a doctrine, reserving the right to display our desire, and sharing what works.

In the end, it is quite simple. Stop and listen. Take control. Chain and master whatever is holding you back and make it your steed to ride upon.

For the mystery of lawlessness is already at work, but only until the one who now restrains it is removed.

BORGES

From his spoken word and personality

Prologue

When one is in the presence of a master, there exists the natural tendency to want to challenge him. To take the rules he established and to break them. That is, of course, for a certain kind of artist, bent on being not just different but *more* than anything and anyone that has come before. There is also the loyalist way, the way of absorption, and the way of the researcher, the one who will delve into origins.

In the case of Borges, this would have us delving into Dante's Divine Comedy, which was for Borges the beginning and the end of literature, in some way, and to which he would never cease referring. We would have to take a look at Walt Whitman and Sir Thomas Browne for a beginning, at Schopenhauer as an engine running in the background throughout his life, as well as William James, Herbert Spencer, and Henri Bergson standing guard behind Borges' father.

We could, however, also understand the development of the genius of art as a gift. Rather than tread the ground Borges has covered and relearn the things that he distinguished through a life dedicated to acute perception, we could simply take those things without worrying where they came from, or how he came to them. Perhaps, we could, instead, take off where he left off. The place he was at when he wrote his final insights into Dante's work, and his last four short stories.

Throughout the text, we explore a relationship with a late Borges who adhered to nothing but an organic flow, an honest and settled-down expression, and a serenity in being oneself. This is the Borges who admired the cold calm of Confucius and the dreamy mystery of the surviving works written in Old Norse.

The following are some essays that part from comments that Borges made during interviews, notably during his late 70s interviews. In these, we can hear a side of Borges that does not come through in his writing, in which he tends to be very formal. Occasionally, we get glimpses of it in his prepared oral lectures, such as in *Siete Noches*. But it is during interviews that we see his full wit and playfulness come through with a sharpness that is never manifest elsewhere. It is in conversation that his intellect looms over topics, puzzling us not just for what he says, but what he keeps silent about, and the way he does this.

Most of the essays here take Borges' comments as parting point and then make references to passages from other writers and old works to enrich and move the discussion forward. We hope that you will find great pleasure in reading them and sharing your opinions on each of the essays.

The artist's work is one

Borges once said that everything he would eventually write was contained in *Fervor de Buenos Aires*. Published in 1923, this work of poetry showed us the mind of a young Borges exploring his predilections of form and theme. His admiration for Walt Whitman comes through, as well as his intention to remain 'contemporary', an idea he later disowned, stating that one cannot help but be what one is.

Everything he would ever write was there, except said in between the lines, and only for himself, he said. He went on to say nobody could see it except for himself. We suppose he means that nobody would have been able to see it when he first published it. In hindsight, and as a third party, such things are quite evident. His publishing of *Evaristo Carriego*, the references to "el *Martín* Fierro", the constant references to Buenos Aires, and his never-ending praise for Walt Whitman would remain some of his prominent features to those who saw beyond the "labyrinths, clocks, and puzzles".

It has been said, Borges tells us, that we are what we are, and that we discover ourselves through experience, in a constant search. The search of the artist, which is none other than the search of the individual, of the human being, is taken up in a unique way for each person. In our view, there have been three great mages of Iberian-American art, all incompatible with each other, one of them a pariah by virtue of his affiliations, yet all of them belonging to a higher order of intelligence and power of creation.

For the Chilean Alejandro Jodorowsky, the path took the form of living a surrealist life, performing for a moving theater, becoming one with the Tarot, and living a Zen-oriented life, always following his heart and an ideal of doing good for humanity. For Jodorowsky's compatriot and spiritual opposite, Miguel Serrano, the path took him down a story right out of Novalis' mind, fusing the mystique of Hermann Hesse with the archetypal psychology of Carl Gustav Jung, mythologizing Adolf Hitler, filtering and interpreting Pythagorean hints through Plato, and amalgamating Wolfram's *Parzival* with the Order SS Black Sun ideal.

For Borges, it took the shape of the secretive Cabalistic sorcerer, inhabiting libraries as if possessed by the collective souls of the authors housed in the thousands upon thousands of volumes, consulting and consorting with Jewish intellectuals, early on authoring essays with titles such as "A Defense of the Kabbalah" and "I, a Jew", and subsequently publishing diminutive works that changed the course of literature during the time he lived, and beyond.

Borges, who cultivated a love for Germanic languages, especially for the ancient ones, might have empathized with the following passage from the Anglo-Saxon poem *The Wanderer*:

Oft him anhaga — are gebideð,
metudes miltse, þeah þe he modcearig
geond lagulade longe sceolde
hreran mid hondum hrimcealde sæ,
wadan wræclastas. Wyrd bið ful aræd!

The prose translation of N. Kershaw reads as follows:
"The solitary man is constantly looking for mercy and God's compassion, though over the watery ways with gloomy heart he has long had to stir with his arms the icy sea, treading. the paths of exile. Fate is absolutely fixed! "

Although Borges was not a religious man, nor even a believer in any sense of the word, we can be sure he understood this parable of the solitary man, looking over vast expanses with a taciturn expression, ready to receive, to contemplate, and walk over paths not often tread by others.

Michel de Certeau wrote in his book *La Fable Mystique*, under the heading "Un liue pour se perdre", that:

À ces témoins anciens et disséminés, d'où sortiront les groupes des « fous du Christ » (yourodivyj) qui circulent sur les places de Moscou du xiv au xvi siècle, je demande quel détournement ils produisent. Non pour capter le secret de leur séduction (y en a-t-il un autre que leur propre ravissement?), mais pour essayer de circonscrire le point de fuite par où ils nous détournent vers un absolu. Il s'agit d'un écart vers un autre pays, où la folle (la femme qui se perd) et le fou (l'homme qui rit) créent le défi d'un délié.

The translation by Michael B. Smith reads:

Of these ancient and widely dispersed witnesses from whom would come the groups of "madmen of Christ" [yourodivyj] who circulated on the public squares of Moscow in the fourteenth to sixteenth centuries, I ask: What change of direction did they bring about? Not to capture the secret of their seduction (is there any other besides their own rapture?), but to try to circumscribe the vanishing point through which they turn us toward an absolute. We have here a turning aside toward another country, in which the madwoman (the woman who loses herself) and the madman (the man who laughs) create the challenge of the unbound.

We contend that the unfolding of Borges' body of work posed a similar challenge to the world. It was not the challenge of mere *form* which Cortázar would take from James Joyce's *Ulysses* and funnel, in spirit, into *Rayuela* and *Libro de Manuel*. It was rather what Cortázar learned that made him a teacher, what he shows us in *Bestiario* or *Las armas secretas*. The art of hinting, of opening spaces, by going into particulars in a way that creates voids that the reader then fills in. It is also the art of implication.

Now, in contrast to Julio Cortázar, or Roberto Bolaño, for that matter, who settle squarely into "lo cotidiano", the day-to-day, Borges includes such personal details, private scenes, as reserved and rather sacred tokens that expand the reader's mind even as they contract. The side-to-side movements of Borges, slow-moving and submerged in an ocean of philosophical silence, have the power to act as a door to other worlds. That ever-present but unseen presence in between the lines of text is what Borges mined through the decades as if for gems. It is also what allowed him to extend an invisible hand over the imaginations of scores of readers. Borges would reach the end of his life with the discrete crowning achievements put forth in *La memoria de Shakespeare* and *Nueve ensayos dantescos*, having touched but a fraction of his universe.

On being ruled

One hopes, Borges said, that one day we deserve not to have any government anywhere in the world. The statement is an enlightened one, founded on the grounds of a liberal anarchism. Not the destructive anarchism most people are familiar with, but the kind coaxed by attitudes founded in principles of higher mind. The same that mislead Scandinavians into thinking people from all over the world are "just the same as we are".

Like most Iberian-Americans, Borges understood well that for democracy to work, people had to have evolved a certain culture, a certain way of being, beyond savagery or the survival impulse that often leads to crassness. The noble savage, we could posit, exists, but it is the exception rather than the rule. For the rest, culture and morals are necessary. Thus, for society to remain ordered and livable, we need either a government that is strong enough in relation to the uncivilized impulses of the masses, or for the masses to have adopted such culture and morals through which their behavior becomes self-regulated.

Confucius, in Book 1 chapter 10 of his Analects, writes:
Tsze-ch'in asked Tsze-kung, saying, 'When our master comes to any country, he does not fail to learn all about its government. Does he ask his information? or is it given to him?' (trans. James Legge)

Several things, or indeed many things, could be said about this passage. First is the implied demeanor of the master, the status or personality that affords him a certain respect, and the transfer of information. Second, the civility pointed to, and which we most willingly take at face value. One of the lessons is the master does not need to wrestle the information, nor even ask it to be given to him directly. He observes, above all, and learns.

While Confucius here is not talking about the absence of government nor do we intend to commit the anachronism of naming him as a precursor of liberal anarchism, we take from it positive ideal. The civility displayed in such a passage, repeated and taught to a student as a lesson back then, was also what Borges loved best of the gentleman ideal. It was also what he admired of the Swiss. That ability to remain neutral, to renounce, as he put it, being Italian, German or French, and to "be something else", in peace with each other.

Henri Bergson writes, in *The Meaning of the War: Life & Matter in Conflict*:

The moral energy of nations, as of individuals, is only sustained by an ideal higher than themselves, and stronger than themselves, to which they cling firmly when they feel their courage waver. (trans. T. Fischer Unwin Ltd. 1915)

This moral energy that Bergson points out could well be what Borges thought was needed for all of us to "deserve" not having any form of government.

We remind the reader that Borges' comment came as a remark upon being asked his views on democracy. He replied he did not much like it, but that he wanted to make it clear he thought that it was possible other countries could very well function with democracy, just not his own. This sentiment is shared by many thinking peoples of Iberian-America.

By way of contrast, Nietzsche writes in *Menschliches, Allzumenschliches* of those who will, despite being strong, not be willing to grasp freedom:

Was bindet am festesten? welche Stricke sind beinahe unzerreissbar? Bei Menschen einer hohen und ausgesuchten Art werden es die Pflichten sein: jene Ehrfurcht, wie sie der Jugend eignet, jene Scheu und Zartheit

vor allem Altverehrten und Würdigen, jene Dankbarkeit für den Boden, aus dem sie wuchsen, für die Hand, die sie führte, für das Heiligthum, wo sie anbeten lernten, - ihre höchsten Augenblicke selbst werden sie am festesten binden, am dauerndsten verpflichten.
The translation by Alexander Harvey reads:
What binds strongest? What cords seem almost unbreakable? In the case of mortals of a choice and lofty nature they will be those of duty: that reverence, which in youth is most typical, that timidity and tenderness in the presence of the traditionally honored and the worthy, that gratitude to the soil from which we sprung, for the hand that guided us, for the relic before which we were taught to pray—their sublimest moments will themselves bind these souls most strongly.

Here, we see Nietzsche making the case that those rules that keep in place or orient Bergson's "moral energy" are but strictures upon the strong. Many people take this as an opportunity to lampoon Nietzsche, to blame him for all those who, freed from such strictures, have deemed themselves at liberty to carry out all manner of savagery. The proper context of this appeal, however, is more in line with Borges than we would think at first.

For Nietzsche, freedom and nobility come from the inside, from intrinsic nature, from untaught tendencies that react to the environment. For him, education cannot bestow a kind and just heart. He sees all repression as an excuse, and a bad one, to restrict the individual. To understand Nietzsche, to discuss him, even cursorily, would take many pages and a long digression, however. Suffice it to say that Borges, as in everything, took a more middle-of-the-road stance, a balanced one in which he championed the right of individual freedom, except where bad actors sought to destroy the very fabric of the society that guaranteed such freedoms.

An unbearably sentimental man

Having been accused of writing in a cold and distant tone of voice, and of not straying from the factual in his stories, Borges replied that such accusations did not have any merit. "Soy", he said, "desagradablemente sentimental." Meaning, he considered himself to be *unpleasantly* sentimental.

The said coldness is more apparent, by the way, in English translation than in the original Spanish. His original writing appears, to the native speaker at any rate, as measured, distant, perhaps, avoiding the pathetic though not altogether the emotional. In Spanish, Borges said he tried to maintain a certain "pudor", that is, a kind of shy reticence, a reluctance to show too much of oneself, but that he was, as a matter of fact, a very sentimental man.

Rubén Darío was an epoch-making Nicaraguan poet who ushered *modernismo* in the Spanish tongue. Hispanic *modernismo* is a distinct and separate event from English language modernism. They both share a common influence in the vast literature of the French, but they drink of that river independently and through the particular relation each language bears to that third tongue. Darío wrote, in his book, *Tierras Solares*, that:

> ¿Quién no se siente en un caso igual poseído de ese tartarinismo sentimental, que sin que notemos a la inmediata su influencia, nos solidariza un tanto con los tipos de nuestras lecturas, con los personajes que nos han hecho pensar y soñar un poco, por la poesía de su vida, que nos liberta por instantes de la prosa de nuestra existencia práctica cuotidiana?

In English:

Who does not feel in the same case possessed by that sentimental Tartarinism, which without us immediately noticing its influence, gives us some solidarity with the types of our readings, with the characters who have made us think and dream a little, for example? the poetry of his life, which frees us for moments from the prose of our daily practical existence?

Like the passionate American, Harold Bloom, Borges, too, had shared in the imaginary lives of thousands of characters, had fallen down the delightful ravines of poetry. Unlike Harold Bloom, however, the aristocrat in Borges lead him to decorous restraint. Observation will yield a secret of the elite, the origin of which has to do with energy preservation, but which through the centuries has devolved into the trappings of "having class". Borges certainly made the most out of each word and hand gesture.

When one looks closely at Borges' writings, we see a man of great passion that refuses to go the whole way. It may be that something else came to his mind and he did not want to get bogged down in the display of what was inside of him. Or it may have been the ploy of one who seeks to keep power to himself.

Dante writes in the 18th Canto of his *Inferno*:
*E quel frustato celar si credette
bassando 'l viso; ma poco li valse,*
The translation by Longfellow reads:
*And he, the scourged one, thought to hide himself,
Lowering his face, but little it availed him;*
Out of clever modesty, Borges would direct negative epithets towards himself to wrangle himself from inopportune questions. He would, for instance, often refer to his limited capacity to see, to do, to understand, and so on. Under it all, the attentive will not be deceived. Under it all, too, the empathetic among us will agree with his tactics, justified by an end in the respect for personal opinion and choice.

At the same time, he was not afraid of saying what he thought. Borges used the above ploy only when interviewers and other interlocutors would attempt to corner him into explaining his preferences. We could say of Borges that he was opinionated but not impertinent, decidedly singular in his views but not insistent that anyone else should accept them.

Nicolás Gómez Dávila writes in his *Escolios a un texto implícito*:
Ser cristianos es hallarnos ante quien no podemos escondernos, ante quien no es posible disfrazarnos.
Es asumir la carga de decir la verdad, hiera a quien hiera.
In English:
To be Christians is to find ourselves before whom we cannot hide, before whom it is not possible to disguise ourselves.
It is to assume the burden of telling the truth, no matter who it hurts.

And such a burden Borges did indeed shoulder. It probably cost him the Nobel Prize. And yet, to such who strike through, and dare speak uncomfortable truths, allies come, protectors arise. Among those of a mentally balanced disposition, even those who did not agree with many of his opinions came to be his admirers and supporters. Because, as Borges once said, a man's opinion is the least important thing about him.

Transforming experience into symbol

The poet never rests, Borges once said. His work is that of constantly transmuting experience into sounds, words, fables, narrative, poetry. Borges had been instructed by his father never to rush the publishing of a work, to write when the time was right, when things came to him. Borges seems to have adhered to those directives for the rest of his life. Doubling down and focusing on what mattered for him, on what most inspired him, on what most delighted him, which included a love of style, astuteness and implied depth, took him far.

Andrés Holguín, referring to Barba-Jacob in his book *Antología Crítica de la Poesía Colombiana*, writes:
La poesía se incuba muy lentamente en el alma del creador y luego es traducida a través de símbolos, giros, signos. Todo ello debe ser asimilado, descifrado.

In English:
Poetry incubates very slowly in the soul of the creator and is then translated through symbols, turns, signs. All of this must be assimilated, deciphered.

In this excellent book delving into the nature of poetry by taking the Colombian poets of a whole century up to 1975 as guide, the author tells us of the same translation of experience into symbols that Borges talks about. He goes further and tells us that, as readers, it is our job to then take those symbols and decode them. To decode them, we must first assimilate them so that we can then decipher their origin.

One is reminded how systems of symbols have been devised that are meant to be memorized in painstaking detail, after which those details must be examined, pondered, and creatively explored. The system of symbols is then absorbed into the psyche and becomes "personalized". That is, each system of symbols will express itself through each individual matrix. Among such systems of symbols are religious myths and folklore, and also the occult systems poured into such devices as the *Tarot de Marseille*.

William James in the sixth and seventh lectures of *The Varieties of Religious Experience*, titled "The Sick Soul", wrote:

Recent psychology has found great use for the word "threshold" as a symbolic designation for the point at which one state of mind passes into another. Thus we speak of the threshold of a man's consciousness in general, to indicate the amount of noise, pressure, or other outer stimulus which it takes to arouse his attention at all.

Thus, in producing such symbols, the artist must assume or generate, through the realization of the work, a degree of interest and fascination that exerted on the mind of the reader, listener, or consumer of such a work surpasses that threshold. It is not enough that your book, music or image is read, or that it is recognized. The fascination it produces among a great number of those who come across it must draw in attention, captivating the mind so that the rest of the world recedes into the background.

Borges pronounced in the "Poetry" lecture of his *Siete Noches*:

La poesía es el encuentro del lector con el libro, el descubrimiento del libro. Hay otra experiencia estética que es el momento, muy extraño también, en el cual el poeta concibe la obra, en el cual va descubriendo o inventando la obra. Según se sabe, en latín las palabras "inventar" y "descubrir" son sinónimas. Todo esto está de acuerdo con la doctrina platónica, cuando dice que inventar, que descubrir, es recordar. Francis Bacon agrega que si aprender es recordar, ignorar es saber olvidar; ya todo está, sólo nos falta verlo.

Translated into English:
Poetry is the reader's encounter with the book, the discovery of the book.

There is another aesthetic experience that is the moment, also very strange, in which the poet conceives the work, in which he discovers or invents the work. As is known, in Latin the words "invent" and "discover" are synonymous. All this is in accordance with the Platonic doctrine, when it says that to invent, to discover, is to remember. Francis Bacon adds that if learning is remembering, ignoring is knowing how to forget; Everything is already there, we just need to see it.

The poet, the writer, the creator, must, per the quoted passage above, *find* the work that mystifies him, that attracts and submerges him in a different dimension. It has been said that the artist must feel engrossed in the work, thereby infusing the symbols within the work with that energy, so that the onlooker can also feel something similar. The hope is that, all of us being human, what fascinates one of us deeply may also fascinate the other. The question of individual differences and preferences arises. What so attracts a majority of human beings must address itself to a universal element, to something in the nervous system, in the reptilian brain, perhaps, without discounting the evolution to which we have been subjected. The evolution, that is, not just of biology, but of manners and culture, of language and morality.

The danger of tapping strongly into the vein of what-is is that one can easily fall into redundancies. We may end up parroting or repeating what has been said *ad nauseam*. But the symbols and the manners, and so on, do not need to be respected, they do not even need to be adhered to. As long as clear reference is made to them, there will be a strong link between producer and consumer. How we choose to play that game of subliminal communication will come to individual choice.

Erring to learn

Borges once said that making mistakes was necessary to learn "astucias y modestias". The first word, as the adjective "astuto", means "cunning", the second is originally a noun meaning "modesty". One learns, in other word, little tricks of cunning and modesty through erring.

For Borges, as for many writers, his early works were trials, drafts, and improvements upon one another, always towards a better realization. But in all of this, at least in hindsight when he pronounced these words, there is an acceptance that the work will not be perfect, and that the author will not be perfect.

Right at the beginning of chapter twenty of the *Dao de jing* (or, more confusingly romanized, *Tao teh king*, roughly meaning *The Way Through Virtue*), we find the following line:

(*Juéxué wú yōu*)

THAT IS, IN DIRECT translation:
To learn absolutely without worries. / Absolute knowledge without worries.

More specifically, because of how "jué" is used, we could say, to learn entirely. Being more free of strictures and scholarship, we could posit "jué" as affecting the whole phrase, to learn without worrying *at all*.

In other words, one keeps learning, one keeps moving forward. Above all, one does not stop and overthink. To learn "absolutely", to absorb not just the craft in its technicalities, but the states of mind and the right physiology, the emotions, perhaps even the right seasons most advantageous to do certain things.

León Dujovne, in the second tome of his work on Spinoza, titled *La época de Baruj Spinoza*, writes the following:

Cuando creemos conocer cosas particulares, nuestro conocimiento no es verdadero; cuando creemos tener una voluntad absolutamente libre, estamos igualmente en error. Verdadero es el conocimiento de Dios y sus atributos; lo es también el de las cosas y de los hechos cuando pensamos en los hechos y en las cosas sul) specie aeternitatis, ligados entre sí por causas y efectos en la unidad de la sustancia divina.

Translated to English:

When we believe we know particular things, our knowledge is not true; When we believe we have an absolutely free will, we are equally in error. True is the knowledge of God and the attributes of him; It is also that of things and facts when we think of facts and things sub specie aeternitatis, linked together by causes and effects in the unity of the divine substance.

The God of Spinoza is, of course, not the God of the Church. We will let someone else be the judge whether his God is the God of the Jews. Following the words, and going beyond Spinoza himself, into a pantheistic conception of God as the universe, as the *conscious* order of causes and effects, knowledge of God may be taken as knowledge of reason. Not the reason of conventional logic, but of the open-minded reason that lead Aristotle, Da Vinci, and Franklin all to *observe* the nature of the universe that surrounded them as it presented itself directly to them.

But, as Chesterton writes in his book *Heretics* regarding the reduction of mysterious and magical places and things in the world to their "understanding":

If we wish to understand them it must not be as tourists or inquirers, it must be with the loyalty of children and the great patience of poets. To conquer these places is to lose them. The man standing in his own kitchen-garden, with fairyland opening at the gate, is the man with large ideas. His mind creates distance; the motor-car stupidly destroys it. Moderns think of the earth as a globe, as something one can easily get round, the spirit of a schoolmistress.

And here we come to the *modesty* of which Borges spoke. The modesty not to prod to the point of destroying the world; the world of imagination, of fascination; the inner world, of which the outer world is but an interpreted reflection, and from which artistic creation and human meaning are derived. The *cunning* of Borges was also one, then, that sought to preserve this modesty. Modesty is the intention, the end, and the cunning is the means to realizing that intention.

Borges might have been referring to much more, nevertheless, and all we have done here is direct it to a relevant point regarding our interpretation of the writer.

There is, we could say, a proper way of making mistakes that leads to that modesty and to that cunning. These are mistakes that burn us, leaving scars on our skin. They are committed by going beyond what is deemed appropriate, by transgressing. Then the backlash comes from reality itself, from our feelings, from the host of spirits that inhabit our limbs and organs.

A book is already too much

Early on, Borges spoke about the excess of writing novels, whole books, when the delight and self-containment of a short story or a collection of interpolated encyclopedic data accomplished the end of entertainment (or informing, choose what you want to call it) better. They do so without the exhaustion and boredom associated with reading long and intricate works.

Showered with compliments in his old age, Borges once answered he could boast of having written "a few valid pages, one or other poem". That was it for him. Enjoyment of depth and variety expressed concisely.

Borges held a passing interest in the Kabbalah. As far as we know, he never learned Hebrew or went into the study of Jewish mysticism in any depth. What interested him were the procedures, the general idea of the Kabbalah, which we could suspect were the salient points. He mentions the reading and interpretative games of the Kabbalah. But what interested him the most was the implication, or rather the precondition, that made *kabbalistic* operations possible in the first place. Scripture, he once wrote, we may imagine as an intelligence that comes into our world in the form of series of letters, the order of which wholly escapes chance.

Gershom Scholem, in his book *Kabbalah*, writes:
Following the pattern of several of the Psalms, the view was developed that the whole of creation, according to its nature and order, was singing hymns of praise.

Each psalm, for any who has taken the time to imbibe their essence, is self-contained. As much as we can study relations between each other, they are complete and can be recited to great effect without a theological background or indoctrination as prerequisite. Inspect, for instance, the potency of Psalm 91 in the King James Version, which many of us raised in the Christian religion are made to memorize:

He that dwelleth in the secret place of the most High shall abide under the shadow of the Almighty. I will say of the LORD, He is my refuge and my fortress: my God; in him will I trust. Surely he shall deliver thee from the snare of the fowler, and from the noisome pestilence. He shall cover thee with his feathers, and under his wings shalt thou trust: his truth shall be thy shield and buckler. Thou shalt not be afraid for the terror by night; nor for the arrow that flieth by day; Nor for the pestilence that walketh in darkness; nor for the destruction that wasteth at noonday. A thousand shall fall at thy side, and ten thousand at thy right hand; but it shall not come nigh thee. Only with thine eyes shalt thou behold and see the reward of the wicked. Because thou hast made the LORD, which is my refuge, even the most High, thy habitation; There shall no evil befall thee, neither shall any plague come nigh thy dwelling. For he shall give his angels charge over thee, to keep thee in all thy ways. They shall bear thee up in their hands, lest thou dash thy foot against a stone. Thou shalt tread upon the lion and adder: the young lion and the dragon shalt thou trample under feet. Because he hath set his love upon me, therefore will I deliver him: I will set him on high, because he hath known my name. He shall call upon me, and I will answer him: I will be with him in trouble; I will deliver him, and honour him. With long life will I satisfy him, and shew him my salvation.

Borges aspired to such conciseness, without having ever compared his work to sacred scripture. He said of his writing that it aimed to entertain rather than persuade, just like *The Thousand and One Nights* (or, as he enjoyed quoting the Richard F. Burton title, *The Thousand Nights and One Night*). Borges, though, and in contrast to the endless flow of the Arabic tales, did aspire to the emphatic pulse of sacred scripture, whenever it suited his fancy.

The trusting of his instinct, a trust one may compare to the "dwelling in the secret place of the most High", which led him to always choose for himself what he desired, what he wished for, may have gradually led to his ascendancy, as if under the charge of angels. Who shall tell?

Seyyed Hossein Nasr, in his An Introduction to Islamic Cosmological Doctrines, writes:

These heavenly souls, or angels, act upon the elements to generate the beings below the sphere of the Moon, in a manner similar to that in which music acts upon the human soul.

Again, we hear the echo of musical acts of creation, of acting through the laws of harmony (and, of necessity, disharmony), overshadowed, or generated, by creatures of the heavens. The Islamic doctrine would give its laws and tenor to the Kabbalah that Gershom Scholem describes above. The Kabbalah inherits Islamic cosmology and Christian-Gnostic mysticism, funneled through the lens of Jewish religious aesthetic.

Ignacio Cabral writes, in *Los símbolos cristianos,* that:

La imagen histórico-descriptiva (o narrativa) se destina a la trasmisión del mensaje cristia- no: escenas de la vida de Cristo, figuras del Antiguo Testamento, etc. Responde a un programa de instrucción y evangelización, muy útil para educar a los fieles en la Historia Sagrada. Fue necesaria cuando los libros eran escasos y había muchos ignorantes y analfabetas. En la actualidad, este tipo de imágenes ya no tienen sentido con los nuevos medios de comunicación, pero se reserva a los analfabetas y a los que necesariamente necesitan de este tipo de representaciones.

In English:

The historical-descriptive (or narrative) image is intended for the transmission of the Christian message: scenes from the life of Christ, figures from the Old Testament, etc. It responds to a program of instruction and evangelization, very useful for educating the faithful in Sacred History. It was necessary when books were scarce and there were many ignorant and illiterate women. Currently, these types of images no longer make sense with the new media, but are reserved for the illiterate and those who necessarily need this type of representations.

Like so, Borges, without imposing his opinion as a dictum upon the world of literature, came to think that the novel, the full-length book, was too much. We may come to agree with him in view of the rapid pace of the modern world, the piecemeal way in which we are forced to consume everything. We end up partitioning our consumption of everything into bits that are of necessity interlaced with many engineered fictions from our technological world in a way that was unknown to humans one hundred years ago. The shift happened across Borges' lifetime, and his work expresses that shift wonderfully.

Once something is written

I do not think about an audience, I try to express what I wish to say, and I try doing so in the simplest possible way, Borges said. Once something has been written, it is already outside of me. That is, out of his hands, no longer, also, a part of him.

Borges had a very clear conception of personal space. For him, as for many other anarchic-minded people such as Jodorowsky, there are no groups, there are only individuals. We have our opinions, and what others do with them is their business. Now, whereas Jodorowsky is a phoenix of creativity, Borges sought the more discrete road. Whereas Jodorowsky exploded into vitality and a variety of beings beyond Jung or Shakespeare, Borges focused his willpower on the sacred letters, through a careful contemplation of what he and the world was.

Zhuang Zi (or Chuang Tzu) quotes Lao Zi (Lao Tzu) saying: *"The snow-goose is white without a daily bath. The raven is black without daily colouring itself. The original simplicity of black and of white is beyond the reach of argument. The vista of fame and reputation is not worthy of enlargement. When the pond dries up and the fishes are left upon dry ground, to moisten them with the breath or to damp them with a little spittle is not to be compared with leaving them in the first instance in their native rivers and lakes." (Trans. Herbert A. Giles)*

As Borges aged, not only did he seek to express himself simply, as if he were speaking, and thereby exalting oral speech, but he was more comfortable being himself. Distinctly from his younger self, he also did not feel the need to try and be modern, contemporary, or regional. You are what you are. You cannot help but be what you are. To pretend to be otherwise, or to pretend to be what you already are, is just a complication.

In the Poetic Edda, strophe 30 of the Harbarthsljoth (The Poem of Harbarth), we read:
> "Ek vas austr ok viþ einhverja dǿmþak,
> lēk ek viþ ena līnhvítu ok launþing hāþak,
> gladdak ena gollbjǫrtu, gamni mǽr unþi."

Henry Adams Bellows translates:
> "Eastward I was, and spake with a certain one,
> I played with the linen-white maid, and met her by stealth;
> I gladdened the gold-decked one, and she granted me joy."

The simplicity of both Eddic poetry and ancient Chinese philosophy entranced the aged Borges. It spoke of a soft-walking, of a hand stretched out to feel the morning dew, of the joy of contemplating the world, of choosing for oneself. In late life, the liberal anarchist ideals of the father, and for which he stood all of his life, blossomed into quietude, into perfect introspection.

Sadly, we never see in Borges more than little inventions, penetrating and instigating as they are. No sign that he felt his soul visited or elevated by something else. This, despite his rather reserved admiration for Novalis and, even more so, for Angelus Silesius.

It is possible that Borges sought to un-name, within himself, the characterizations, the anthropomorphization of that which Angelus Silesius, and perhaps himself, felt and perceived. A vibrant world, a chaotic world, streamlined into sense and reason through consciousness. Made beautiful and ordered, made *necessary*, by human will. Not the will that tills the land, but the pure will of the mystic mind, the apprehension of what in Spanish is called "mística" ("mystique" in French) and for which no translation or precise concept exists in English.

William James writes, in his book Pragmatism: A new name for some old ways of thinking:

'Energy' is the collective name (according to Ostwald) for the sensations just as they present themselves (the movement, heat, magnetic pull, or light, or whatever it may be) when they are measured in certain ways. So measuring them, we are enabled to describe the correlated changes which they show us, in formulas matchless for their simplicity and fruitfulness for human use. They are sovereign triumphs of economy in thought.

Such energy, the attentive recollection of the world through the senses, led Borges also to that "economy of thought" that is is palpable throughout his work, and which intensifies into a fine and sharp edge into his late work. Borges, especially in his work after 1975, cannot be captured in rapid reading. One does not capture him by inhaling the mist surrounding his work, as one could with his works from the '40s and '50s. We must *enter the line*, feel around the contours of statements, which are seldom descriptions. Here, when he gave the most of himself, he gave you also the opportunity to make it yours.

The spoken word

"Solamente las palabras del lenguaje oral tiene eficacia", Borges said. Only the language of everyday conversation, of intimate connection, can be effective. He continued to illustrate by pointing out that not all of the words you find in the dictionary can be used. Many words in a dictionary are there for documentary purposes. They may catalog the full range of the language, even the strangest and most regional expressions, or those that have long gone out of use and that nobody recognizes anymore.

One must write, Borges went on, with the language of conversation, or with the language of intimacy. But to that, one arrives in time. That is, a certain experience, a certain self-knowledge, and a certain peace, are necessary.

It used to be that an elaborate language heavy on Latinisms dominated the English tongue. It was good taste to write like Edward Gibbon or Edmund Burke. In our opinion, it continues to be good taste to write like them. They exemplified the greatest natural and flowing expression within that neo-classic paradigm of Western European letters. In time, what is deemed tasteful switched to a more toned-down selection of letters.

Now, it would be easy to mislead ourselves into thinking that this was a matter of heavy latinate versus more indigenous Briton words, or older words, more in line with the language. But good and bad taste writers have existed in every period of time whether they adhere to contemporary notions of written language or cling desperately to the archaic.

When we try and explore Borges' idea, and take in a wider context, especially his love of tasteful English writers such as Gibbon and De Quincey, we understand that efficacy is not just one of logical communication. Language does not just get across the strict meaning of words. Words, as has been said, are shared experiences. What the dictionary says about those words is not enough. What one group or other says about them does not suffice. Above all, words are an individual-to-individual bridge, not a writer-to-masses one, though individuals may indeed derive their personal meanings from group-shared ones. Words transmit feelings and states of mind.

Regarding taste, Roberto Calasso, in his *La Rovina di Kasch*, in the chapter "Sul Gusto" writes:

Ma la sorgente del gusto è un'altra: gusto è ora il contrassegno dell'iniziazione: si applica a tutto e a nulla in particolare, è un sigillo dell'esistenza, la sostituzione definitiva di una sapienza che è di buon gusto non ricordare neppure.

In English:

But the source of taste is another: taste is now the mark of initiation: it applies to everything and nothing in particular, it is a seal of existence, the definitive replacement of a wisdom that it is in good taste not even to remember.

That is, taste, like many things that the aristocracy has codified as markers of worth are vestiges of more organic ways of perception that constituted a *wisdom*. You see someone talk a certain way, and you realize this is an indicator. A certain inclination to use their bodies, their words, a certain way, gives them away as "displeased" or "trapped in obsessions". Wisdom would dictate, be wary of this person, they are not in control of themselves. And, one would presume, the marker of an ascendant aristocracy is its capacity and talent for control, starting with self-control or, more appropriately, self-direction.

It may or may not define the person as a whole. According to certain up-to-date psychology quarters, this is not the case. The sense of self, that is, consciousness, is separate from *nervous system states* which are the causes of those indicators. There is an argument to be made for inherited curses, for inherited *class*, as we now know that epigenetics are inherited. The role of the epigenome is to interpret and translate the DNA code into actual instructions. The epigenome determines physiology Moreover, epigenetics are heavily influenced by what has come to be termed "environment". Environment is not just "what happens to the individual", but *how the individual has chosen to react.*

We are not forwarding an idea of implicit fault, or anything similar to the idea of the karmic rebirth of Vaishnavism, where even the most seemingly innocent individual is receiving the backlash of previous life actions. The way a child is treated during infancy can be embedded into its nervous system. It affects the whole of physiology, and may even, some argue, remain permanently embedded in the epigenome and inherited to future generations. This is what generational trauma consists of.

José Ortega y Gasset, for his part, writes, in the preliminar note to his *La idea de principio en Leibniz y la evolución de la teoría deductiva*:

Pero Nietzsche nos recuerda que Sísyfo —de sophós— con reduplicación, quiere decir el sabio, Sapiens, y este vocablo lo mismo que su doble griego no quiere decir erudito ni hombre de ciencia, sino más simplemente el que distingue de «sabores», de sapideces, el catador, el que tiene buen paladar; en suma, el hombre de buen gusto.

In English:

But Nietzsche reminds us that Sisyphus —from sophós— with reduplication, means the wise man, Sapiens, and this word, like its Greek double, does not mean scholar or man of science, but more simply the one who distinguishes among "flavors", among things which are tasteful, the taster, the one who has a good palate; in short, the man of good taste.

The truly thinking man, in the ancient Greek sense, is not the modern scholar, the man who seeks to understand the world through writings. Rather, it is the one who *can see*, moreover, the one who *can taste*. Studies, upbringing, and so on, can guide, can refine, but they cannot readily impart the capacity. It has been said, therefore, that nothing is teachable. You can only be shown the way or discover it on your own. Such is the nature of good taste as wisdom, independent of inherited class, though taste itself *can* be inherited.

Mircea Eliade writes in *Myth and Reality*:

Through culture, a desacralized religious universe and a demythicized mythology formed and nourished Western civilization-that is, the only civilization that has succeeded in becoming exemplary. There is more here than a triumph of logos over mythos. The victory is that of the book over oral tradition, of the document-especially of the written document over a living experience whose only means of expression were preliterary.

In that triumph of the book over oral tradition the West lost something. It lost tradition, and it came under the spell of the magical object, even as it rejected all ideas of magic. Words as magic had been heavily controlled throughout the Aryan and pre-Aryan tradition, contained in orally memorized poems, later in runes, and finally in codes of law sculpted into rock. It is with the obsession with "books" and "sources" that sensitivity is lost. The reference is no longer your senses and learning how to use them, but what has been written which automatically becomes authority.

The Borges of the 1980s reminds us of the magic of the intimate connection, of the spontaneous words that arise in that setting. All else, as he discusses, everything else we impose on those words, on those emotions, are barriers set between people.

A barrier between writer and reader

Borges confessed to have indulged in a Baroque style of writing when he was younger. He admitted that this was an exercise in vanity. A younger writer, he said, tends to the baroque because he does not feel that what he has to say is worth in and of itself. Thus the arrogance of the grand style. Baroque construction is an arrogance. His interlocutor at the time, the Spanish interviewer Joaquín Soler Serrano added, "there is something like a plea". Borges, ever the gracious conversationalist, conceded that Soler Serrano's phrase was better, and continues, "something like the demand of a tribute, which is worse", and that both things, in any case, are displeasing.

The Reina-Valera 1960 translation of the Bible, in the Book of Isaiah, chapter 14, verse 11, reads:

Descendió al Seol tu soberbia, y el sonido de tus arpas; gusanos serán tu cama, y gusanos te cubrirán.

The King James Version of the Bible reads:

Thy pomp is brought down to the grave, and the noise of thy viols: the worm is spread under thee, and the worms cover thee.

Several interpretations could be elucidated from this passage in relation to what Borges discussed. We could say that arrogance and pomp, as the King James version puts it, brings you closer to death, perhaps through provocation, or perhaps through other, more subtle circumstances. We could also go with the more conventional wisdom that reminds people that they will take nothing to the grave.

Rafael Cansinos-Assens, whom Borges met in his young years in Spain and whose memory he continued to revere to the end of his days, shared, in a collection of extracts from the Talmud he published under the title of *Bellezas del Talmud*, the following extract:

Malvado —me dije a mí mismo—, ¿a qué entregarte en brazos de un mundo que no es el tuyo? ¿Te parece que está bien la vanidad por cosa que será pasto de gusanos y montón de polvo?

In English:

Evil one, I said to myself, why give yourself over to the arms of a world that is not yours? Do you think it's okay to be vain for something that will be food for worms and a pile of dust?

In this passage, we hear the echo of that same idea, that we do not take anything to the grave, and that time will rust all away, that worms will devour all organic matter. But we also find something else. We find the reference to our own otherworldly nature. The passage talks about this world as not being ours. One could write books on that alone.

The baroque style is an edifice of traditional contraptions. Ingenious inventions streamlined into mechanisms. When a creator relies on these alone, as the "young writer" Borges talks about, he does so to cover over a feeling of lack, a shyness that impedes communication to take place. The Baroque, Borges said, comes between two people. But what if the Baroque is only the symptom?

Paul Groussac observes in *La lengua emigrada*:

La enumeración de Proust de objetos y conocimientos —biblioteca, pasado, erudición, etimología, aristocracia—, sorprende por el hecho de dejar el modo filológico como ausencia necesaria que explica a los demás. Explica lo que es una biblioteca en términos de una metáfora sobre la cultura arcaica, lo que es una aristocracia en su modo de conocimiento, lo que es la erudición como salvación absurda de los idiomas ya usados, de la etimología como forma oculta de la filología.

Which, translated to English, reads:

Proust's enumeration of objects and knowledge—library, past, erudition, etymology, aristocracy—is surprising in that it leaves the philological mode as a necessary absence that explains the others. Explains what a library is in terms of a metaphor about archaic culture, what an aristocracy is in its mode of knowledge, what erudition is as an absurd salvation of languages already used, of etymology as a hidden form of philology.

In the context of our discussion, we are not using Groussac's observation as an indictment of Proust. Rather, Proust's method of decoding the objects that signify aristocracy, and tradition tells us of the Baroque interpolation Borges would later oppose in the written language.

What if the trappings of aristocracy have come to deepen the great alienation that exists between them and "the people"? Where once the aristocracy were beloved leaders, untouchable because they exhibited super normal abilities of thought, of precaution, of calculation, and so on, and not because of some law or edict, much later the *idea of separation* was upheld artificially, with void fanaticism that could make you lose your hand to the royal guard for touching the elite.

In this procession of lost wisdom, vestigial attachment to the *indicators* of wisdom, and subsequent infantile conceitedness, the rise to power of the merchant class came to pass. The inheritors of aristocratic perks forgot the mark of aristocracy was the power to act from a superior plane. They forgot the only "divine right" came from effective action, and was not bestowed from without. They remained distracted and engrossed with the *artifacts* of aristocracy, with the playthings of time. The wolves came because the guardians were long gone, and their children had lost all touch with reality. More importantly, they had lost touch with humanity, with the world, and remained trapped in the Baroque world of *concepts*, of beauty not of the world but of an empty *ideal*, drifting in an ocean of self-made suffering.

Borges urges us to look past such edifices, and to reconnect with what is essential, with what is intimate. It starts with the words we choose, and it manifests in works that represent the genuine individual.

I don't try to please anyone

Borges was not known as a people pleaser. In a radio interview, the Argentinian writer Alberto Laiseca said Borges liked to say "cosas malvadas", evil things, such as saying that while everyone enjoyed talking about how much they liked Goethe, he did not like Goethe because he had *actually* read him. "I know," Borges said, "that when I say these things, I do not make new friends ("me enemisto con mucha gente"), but I do not try to make friends nor enemies." Borges said that he simply tried to say what he thought, and that this often led him to indiscretion.

We could forward the idea that the man that exists *sub specie aeternitatis* must of necessity remain sincere. That man, will insist on being who he is, on delivering what he thinks is the truth, to the best of his knowledge and ability. We are, of course, interpreting, decoding, what the situation with Borges might have been.

Alfonso Reyes wrote, in his essay, "De los proverbios y sentencias vulgares", in his *Intenciones*, that:

Alguna virtud existe en lo que es tan extremadamente sincero, en todo aquello que asume aspectos de espontaneidad, cuando así se le dedican las más lentas, las más laboriosas, las más delicadas especulaciones literarias.

The English translation is:

Some virtue exists in what is so extremely sincere, in everything that assumes aspects of spontaneity, when the slowest, the most laborious, the most delicate literary speculations are dedicated to it.

Alfonso Reyes attributes to spontaneity the value of being very amenable to literary investigation. But, from something being interesting, inviting discussion, to being authentic or even desirable, there is a certain distance.

There are other, more nuanced, perspectives.

Nicolás Gómez Dávila writes, in his *Escolios a un texto implícito* that:

La autenticidad rara vez se confunde con la sinceridad espontánea.

La espontaneidad suele ser eco de voces ajenas.

Which translated to English reads:

Authenticity is rarely confused with spontaneous sincerity.

Spontaneity is usually an echo of other people's voices.

Thus, indiscretions in themselves might just be a lack of self-restraint, and not necessarily the mark of authenticity. To be sure, his many opinions did pit Borges, despite the great acclaim he received, against many others in the world. All this, even though he often framed his opinions as being just that, his opinion, and despite the fact that he was always polite about it.

As to Gómez Dávila's opinion that "spontaneity is usually the echo of other people's voices", one would have to question the very truthfulness of the statements that come through when Borges "slips". But the case could also be made that Borges delighted in playing this game. When he was stinging, he was not being spontaneous, he was not "slipping" but was expressing closely held views he developed across a lifetime cultivating discernment and *taste*.

Borges allowed himself to be what he was, and famously restrained himself from attempting things that simply did not appeal to him, despite the acclaim he would have had from doing them.

Angelus Silesius, for whom Borges expressed admiration in his late years, writes, in his *Cherubinischem Wandersmann*, the following:

Was Gott ist, weiß man nicht: Er ist nicht Licht, nicht Geist,

Nicht Wahrheit, Einheit, Eins, nicht was man Gottheit heißt,

Nicht Weisheit, nicht Verstand, nicht Liebe, Wille, Güte,
Kein Ding, kein Unding auch, kein Wesen, kein Gemüte.
A rough and artless translation of the passage above:
We don't know what God is: He is not light, not spirit,
Not truth, unity, oneness, not what is called deity,
Not wisdom, not understanding, not love, will, goodness,
Not a thing, not an absurdity, not a being, not a mind.

Most patently, Borges did not seem to consider himself Argentinean, not because he considered himself to be from somewhere else, but just because he did not seek identification with labels. At the same time, he embraced the particularities of where he was born, how he was raised, and the preferences that his personality developed. He embraced them not as things that defined him per se, not as strictures within which he *must* remain, or as an organic law to which he had to consciously defer. Rather, he just accepted the flow of experience and consciousness, asking of others to let him remain an individual, something he, too, generously awarded others.

On realizing his destiny

Borges said that he discovered his destiny in a tacit manner, and that this was the only way of indicating something. Things must be, he said, assumed. What we may understand from this is that nothing was said to him. The way he sums it up saying that things can only be revealed when you assume them to be true reminds us also of the way human psychology works. That is, if you are not open to the possibility of something, you are not likely to see how it can be true. By becoming open to it, on the other hand, you allow for signs to guide you.

When writing *Evaristo Carriego*, Borges used the word "destino" many times. It does not seem to have been a purposeful keyword nor an explicit theme for him. He just happened to use the word again and again. In the prologue, he says that although he had this fascination with the world of truants out there on the street, he came to realize, despite his illusions, that he grew up not with the subjects of tangos and milongas, but secluded in the garden of his childhood home. He then adds:

¿Qué destinos vernáculos y violentos fueron cumpliéndose a unos pasos de mí, en el turbio almacén o en el azaroso baldío?

Which in English could be translated as:

What vernacular and violent destinies were fulfilled a few steps from me, in the murky warehouse or in the hazardous wasteland?

We note the baroque style of his youth (he was thirty-one years of age at the time he published this work), the use of difficult to translate phrases such as "azaroso baldío", which could also be rendered as "(random) happenstance (vacant) lot (of land)", but that would break the rhythm and weight of the English sentence.

In his *Prosas Profanas*, the Nicaraguan poet Rubén Darío includes a poem by the title of "Divagación". In it, he includes the following verses:

> Ámame en chino, en el sonoro chino
> De Li-Tai-Pe. Yo igualaré a los sabios
> Poetas que interpretan el destino;
> Madrigalizaré junto a tus labios.

Which in rough prose-like English translation say the following:
> Love me in Chinese, in the sound of (the) Chinese
> Of Li-Tai-Pe. I will equal the wise
> Poets who interpret destiny;
> I will make madrigals next to your lips.

As always, there is a hint of frivolity and litheness mixed in with the honey-like textures of Darío's verses, which nevertheless cannot but strike a deep cord. He speaks of destiny interpreted by poets. He refers to the moment of sensual rapture in which melodious lines come naturally to the mind, of impossible foreign tongues, alien cultures replete with great wisdom, dreamy somatic ecstasy. Destiny, or hints of it, only shows itself fleetingly, in between the lines, in the in-between of moments, moments liminal and beyond grasp.

Borges, unlike the majority of other artists, never sought to create a masterpiece. Unlike what you come to expect from "the artist", he strove for *pleasing his soul,* and the key to his name and legacy is that it just happened that his soul had great depth. No perfection or ideal, he admitted to his own cowardice and laziness in the undertaking of immense works. He might have also been deflecting, throwing people off the trail by calling himself names, a technique he often used to get people off his case.

Borges focused on creating what he enjoyed the most. On the little stories and inventions that delighted him in their realization and craft, and also in the final delight that this creation would have for him. He wrote slowly and pondering every line. "Think of the work and not of its fruit," as has been paraphrased and deducted from the second chapter of the Bhagavad Gita.

If we follow Borges' idea that destiny is found in tacit admission, assumption of how things could turn out, we can also find hints of restitution in Jodorowsky's Psychomagic. The idea that things, whatever we feel about them, true or false, must be acted out in a "psycho-drama" as Anton LaVey, founder of the Church of Satan, would put it.

Roberto Bolaño, writing in the context of how a universal work of art is one that can be understood no matter how disfiguring the translation or disastrous its enactment, writes:

Algo similar sucede con las representaciones populares de la Pasión. Esos voluntariosos actores improvisados que una vez al año escenifican la crucifixión de Cristo y que emergen del ridículo más espantoso o de las situaciones más inconscientemente heréticas montados en el misterio, que no es tal misterio, sino una obra de arte.

In English:

Something similar happens with popular representations of the Passion. Those willing improvised actors who once a year stage the crucifixion of Christ and who emerge from the most frightening ridicule or the most unconsciously heretical situations mounted on the mystery, which is not such a mystery, but a work of art.

He is, of course, not referring to professional theater actors, but to the religious ecstasy feasts traditional in Latin America, in which people will participate in processions in honor of Christ and the Virgin. Processions which, if seen by anthropologists who study ancient worldwide cults, would readily summon up the idea of divine possession.

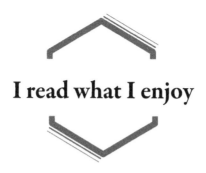

I read what I enjoy

"My father," Borges said, "never told me that Don Quixote was a great work. No, he allowed me to open Don Quixote and read it. He never discussed literature with me. I did not compare books. *Don Quixote* was not, for me, better than *La Hormiga Blanca*. I only enjoyed books. It is possible I was wiser back then, when I enjoyed books rather than now when I try to judge them."

A great deal of Borges' reputation is cemented on the power of his critical eye. Those perspicacious enough also learn that this does not mean that we must absorb his opinions and tout them as our own. Borges boasts of the followers and admirers from the most contrasting and far-flung corners of style, belief and politics. That, despite the fact that he was an avowed old-school liberal with anarchist tendencies who, given the times, fell by default with Conservatism, something that has never ceased to engender controversy and misunderstanding among those who call "Fascism" anything to the right of extreme Marxism.

Whatever the case, he started out his life, as he has recounted, with the mere enjoyment of books. At what point he went from enjoying to judging, it is not certain. We do know that he spent some time as young man in Spain around the respected man of letters Rafael Cansinos-Assens. Cansinos-Assens was mainly known as a translator and literary critic. Although he produced some original works, his reputation was built on his knowledge of languages and his deep sensitivity for the work of art.

Borges would later straddle a middle way between the way of the critique and that of the artist. The tension within him resulting from an overload of understanding and the urge to create resulted in his creation of a unique form. The greatest influence on his work would be the joy he found in reading encyclopedias. The fascination of intersected information from wildly different sources and opinions, more free back then than now when the oppressive hand of forced consensus squashes the possibility of alternate views. He would, toward the end of his life, reconnect with the joy of what one prefers. "At this point," he once said, "I do not read anything new, I only re-read."

William Blake writes of "A Memorable Fancy" in *The Marriage of Heaven and Hell*:

As I was walking among the fires of Hell, delighted with the enjoyments of Genius, which to Angels look like torment and insanity, I collected some of their proverbs, thinking that as the sayings used in a nation mark its character, so the proverbs of Hell show the nature of infernal wisdom better than any description of buildings or garments.

We are reminded of the old saying, that what is pleasing to one man may be off-putting to another, although it is often said in other words. The treading of his own sensitivity, trapped also in his own obsessions and fears, generated the middle-period works that made Borges famous. Those words that came out between 1935 and 1970, most of all. Works that obsess about technique, about detail, about the right inception of veracity.

Borges' short stories cannot be pegged to one genre of fiction or another. If one looks closely, his fiction reads closer to his essays and his poems than it does to other fiction. It is also quite hard to "follow in his footsteps" without taking on the appearance of a counterfeit Borges.

There was always a hint of playful deception in his writing and his words, but you must see the twinkle in his eyes, and know something of a cross section of occult thought and history to grasp it well. He would constantly make reference to detective stories, yet very few of the stories published under his real name fell under that category. Even when they did, there was something of the English fantastical story, yet in Borges it was always more restrained. The secret of Borges is far more atomic than it would seem. But that atomic seed contains only the potential which he actualized by taking strategic lessons from the best fantasy in English literature, the effect of interpolated information gleamed from glancing at encyclopedias, the magical waterfall effect of traditional fairy tales such as the "Arabian Nights", and his own way of convincing the reader that what he is reading is very real indeed.

Gómez Dávila writes the following, regarding pleasure, in the first tome of his *Escolios a un texto implícito*:

El placer es el relámpago irrisorio del contacto entre el deseo y la nostalgia.

Roughly translated to English, the above reads:

Pleasure is the laughable lightning of contact between desire and nostalgia.

The word "laughable" might not be a precise translation, but it gets the work done here. The passage shows Gómez Dávila's typical cynicism which is not inherited, as some could posit, from the likes of Emil Cioran, since they are contemporaries. The work of both appears tinged with a dark and dry knowing. For Gómez Dávila, as per this passage, pleasure is an affair of the memory. "Desire and nostalgia", wanting, longing something that is not any longer. Like so, Borges, like those who delight the deepest in literature, find themselves engrossed and carried away to worlds that are no longer, to worlds that never were.

On writing well

Borges relates an episode with Ernesto Sábato. They discuss the attack under which Cervantes and Dostoyevsky have both come under as "bad writers". Then they make the redundant but no less poignant comment that if writing "badly" they produced a *Don Quixote* and a *Crime and Punishment*, then they did not write so poorly after all. Borges says that although Quevedo or Lope de Vega could have corrected a page from *Don Quixote*, they would not have been able to write it. He says that to correct a page is easy, but to write it is very difficult.

We remind the many that the best and most signal pages from Beckett, no matter what rationalists have to say, come from the "worst" of the "Three Novels" (*Molloy, Malone Dies, The Unnamable*) and, even more so, from the static circular nonsense (more commonly labeled as "absurd") of *Waiting for Godot* and *Texts for Nothing*. That for all his ordered narrative in *Murphy*, and all his genius in his early short stories, which do deserve attention, it is in genuine defiance that he finds that breakthrough, whatever one may make of it.

We say the above in defiance of Borges' own tastes, who we now know utterly despised Beckett's work, and had, in private at least, a manner of contempt for the nature of Joyce's work. Nevertheless, we go beyond Borges' opinion and take it as a sounding board and departure point to explore the relationship between what is considered correct writing versus what has impact.

One more example, and one which the hoity-toity might not approve of, is that of J.K. Rowling's *Harry Potter* books. The books were and continue to be a massive success, even twenty years after their inception. We could argue all day, just as Harold Bloom very publicly did, that this is not real literature. Then again, Bloom also looked down on Jane Austen's *Pride and Prejudice*, which is a roller coaster of precision and wit that keeps on giving. Nevertheless, the *Harry Potter* books command the imaginations and emotions of millions through simple and cartoon-like characterizations, reflecting the simplistic good-and-evil view that most people would wish for. It is a mirror also of a curious the sympathetic and totemic magic world many humans secretly long for, in the back of their minds.

It has been said by readers of *Harry Potter* in Spanish that, having later perused the novels in the original, they think that the quality of the language in translation is much better. That in the original, words and expressions become repetitive, certain rhythms can even be annoying. Skillful translation straightens those wrinkles and delivers a more polished text. Going back to Cervantes and Dostoyevsky, none of this is to say that the translators could have written a *better* version of the *Harry Potter* books. More importantly, the psychological rapture that these books were for the masses was not in any way diminished by its paper-thin constructions, repetitive wording, or the all-too-obvious painting of cardboard evil. After all, human society as a whole, no matter the culture, thrives on superficial (even straw man) images of the "good" and the "bad".

Alfonso Reyes writes in *Cuestiones estéticas*:

Dirán los ligeros que este grito intempestivo, extraño a lo gramatical y a lo racional, es enteramente inexplicable. Pero que respondan los poetas, y digan si no es tan intempestivamente como llegan a la conciencia objetos e imágenes, en el calor impaciente de crear.

In English:

Those who are light will say that this untimely cry, strange to the grammatical and the rational, is entirely inexplicable. But let the poets respond, and say if it is not so unexpectedly that objects and images come to consciousness, in the impatient heat of creating.

That storm of creation, we could argue, is precisely what audiences respond to. They do not respond to good grammar and style, which is not to say that too sloppy a presentation will not get dismissed as unprofessional. The audience does not care for the delicate insights and unfolding perfection of Gombrowicz's prose in his *Diary*. The more masochistic readers might be interested in Krasznahorkai's *Satantango*, and probably not the same few who would watch the film by the same name by Bela Tarr. That, despite the fact that the endless winding sentences that have made Krasznahorkai a sensation among boutique literature appreciators is nothing but a return to the 17^h century habit of using comas more than period and wantonly pulsing through what we now consider run-on sentences.

Spanish Nobel Laureate Camilo José Cela commented that Cervantes' *Don Quixote* was "escrito de un tirón", meaning something close to "written in one go". The book is huge, the sentences are verbose, the feeling is that of overabundance. Not only that, but there are *two* such volumes, the second being more quizzical than the first. And yet, it continues to be a bestseller. Like *Crime and Punishment*, despite the fact that it may be hard work and time consuming, people come out transformed, feeling like their lives are different now, in some way. What is more revealing is that, while *Crime and Punishment* feels, to many, like a soul-crushing slab that teaches them something crucial about humanity, about themselves, *Don Quixote* is a book people read and re-read, sometimes without end, despite the ground it treads not being any less profound.

José Ortega y Gasset writes in La deshumanización del arte y las ideas sobre la novela:

Dentro del artista se produce siempre un choque o reacción química entre su sensibilidad original y el arte que se ha hecho ya. No se encuentra solo ante el mundo (...)

In English:

Within the artist there is always a clash or chemical reaction between his original sensibility and the art that has already been made. You are not alone before the world

It is no mystery that the benefit of hindsight confers on the observer the ability to see mistakes, to distinguish possibilities, that the subject in the situation ignored. Once a revolutionary work has been undertaken and accomplished, it is easy to then think of how it could have been better. A Quevedo, as Borges put it, could have corrected a page from *Don Quixote*, but could he have written it? Could he have written something *like it*? Even with the benefit of hindsight, even having Cervantes' work completed to go by, it is likely he would not.

Often enough, what happens with a great work of art, one that touches the hearts of many, and which is also of monumental proportions, makes subsequent artists grate against it. The comparisons they make to the original work have less to do with how they can realize something *like it* than with how they can *defeat it* by revolutionizing what it did or failed to do. Something similar happens to 19th century composers in relation to Beethoven's symphonies. It is a case of falsely cornering yourself into being able to only go against the great work. The infamous dictum "everything has already been done" stems from the same error.

The fringe Argentine writer Alberto Laiseca left us many Jodorowskean (an unfair epithet, since the two artists are contemporaries, but illustrative to the reader, we hope) fragments and images in his novels. This comes from *El jardín de las máquinas parlantes*:

—¿Y yo qué sé, gordo? A lo mejor ese Dios ya ha muerto, pero desde el pasado supo que ibas a necesitarlo y dejó una energía para vos, en forma potencial, con orden de manifestarse sólo cuando fuera tu tiempo.

And, in English:

> *—And what do I know, fat man? Maybe that God has already died, but from the past he knew that you were going to need him and he left an energy for you, in potential form, with the order to manifest only when it was your time.*

In this way, we may think, the artist should also see the masters of the past which he has idolized to the point of confrontation and confusion. Instead, to see the great work of art as a gift, not just to those who would enjoy it and learn from it for life, but to other artists. To think of the energy, as Laiseca puts it, that God leaves for you to it, God, perhaps, as Cervantes or Dostoyevsky. That is not to say they are untouchable, another corner in which to get trapped. It is just to say that what you have found in that work is an open door and a way into a previously foreclosed region, a mysterious region, now yours to explore.

On death

"Death is something that can mark all men," Borges said. "The idea that we are happenstance, that we are passing, has to move anyone who is not entirely insensitive."

This perception consumed Borges, it drove him to a certain view of life and existence that hankered after the "great sleep of death". It could well have been that Borges was not given to say anything that could lead him to people prying into his beliefs. It was simply easier to say that he was an atheist and did not believe in any form of existence after death. That he was not only at peace with that but that he desired it to come sooner rather than later.

Nevertheless, he discussed and portrayed the feeling and experience of perplexity before the notion of man as a mere flicker in the midst of the great darkness. To him, also, neither fame nor power conferred exemption from our mortal fate. To him, who had scoured encyclopedias and gone deep into the annals of civilization and men great and skilled, only to discover that the records of history themselves were indistinguishable from works of fiction.

Roberto Calasso composes the following wonderful passage in *La rovina de Kasch*:

Al momento di accendere il nuovo fuoco per il re Akaf, i sacerdoti destinarono la sorella più piccola del nuovo re a custode del fuoco. Il suo nome era Sali (così almeno la chiamavano, il suo nome intero era Sali-fu-Hamr). Quando Sali sentì che la scelta era caduta su di lei, si spaventò. E allora Sali sentì una grande paura della morte.

And, in English:
When it was time to light the new fire for King Akaf, the priests assigned the new king's youngest sister as guardian of the fire. Her name was Sali (at least that's what they called her, her full name was Sali-fu-Hamr). When Sali heard that the choice had fallen on her, she became scared.
And then Sali felt a great fear of death.

In a way, ignorance of the great reality allows a person to be happier, to live life idly in the face of the horrible maw that shall one day obliterate their bones into fine dust. For someone like Borges, who did indeed become a "guardian of the fire", that Promethean fire of knowledge and awareness, of freedom, reality became all too evident. The human is born into a brief experience of sensuality, a few meaningful events, and accosted by ailments, soon dies.

Not all who have this deep realization react in the same way as Borges. Fleur Jaeggy, the Swiss writer who writes in Italian and widow of Roberto Calasso, chose to center herself in the sensibility of the writings left to us by Christian mystics such as the Germans Meister Eckhart and Hildegard von Bingen, as well as the Italian Angela da Folino. For her, these possess a higher intelligence, higher than that of philosophers, something that escaped Borges altogether.

Fleur Jaeggy writes the following tempestuous lines in *I beati anni del castigo*:
Avevo una certa furia di vivere nel mondo, e gli aloni della morte riguardavano solo il passato. Il futuro erano i cancelli che si aprivano e i muri che diventano tappeti.

Which in English reads:
I had a certain fury to live in the world, and the halos of death only concerned the past. The future was gates opening and walls becoming carpets.

The work in question is a semi-biographical fiction, and it shines through with a cold passion that wants life and yet is able to see it as if from the comfortable seat of an audience. The point of view and tone of voice of Borges betrays exactly the contrary. It is the voice of someone thrown entirely into what he perceives only as chaos, an endless spiral for which cabalists have invented a rhyme and a reason, but which for Borges were only quaint and entertaining fictions.

Unafraid but terribly aware, Walt Whitman's poem "Whispers of Heavenly Death", from *Leaves of Grass*, reads:

> *Whispers of heavenly death murmur'd I hear,*
> *Labial gossip of night, sibilant chorals,*
> *Footsteps gently ascending, mystical breezes wafted soft and low,*
> *Ripples of unseen rivers, tides of a current flowing, forever flowing,*
> *(Or is it the plashing of tears? the measureless waters of human tears?)*
> *I see, just see skyward, great cloud-masses,*
> *Mournfully slowly they roll, silently swelling and mixing,*
> *With at times a half-dimm'd sadden'd far-off star,*
> *Appearing and disappearing.*
> *(Some parturition rather, some solemn immortal birth;*
> *On the frontiers to eyes impenetrable,*
> *Some soul is passing over.)*

Whitman was Borges' idol in early life. The sense of astonishment transmitted and shared without any intention to give it cause or purpose must have struck the young man terribly deep. More so in an age that had entirely dispensed with divinity and subtler aspects of reality.

On learning a language

Borges said that he was very proud of having learned German on his own. He was prouder of his acquiring of German more than any of the other languages he wielded because he acquired it entirely through his own efforts. And the same thing was happening with the study of Anglo-Saxon (Old English) later in life. He adds to this Old Norse, and muses "*Qué música tiene le alemán, eh?*" ("What music German has, huh?").

Gómez Dávila writes, in *Notas I,* that:
Hay cierta belleza, cierta madurez de la inteligencia, que aparecen sólo cuando el espíritu se abandona a su propio movimiento, cuando el esfuerzo se desvanece en una condescendencia perezosa, cuando el pensamiento se engendra en su mismo fluir.

Which, translated to English says roughly the following:
There is a certain beauty, a certain maturity of intelligence, that appears only when the spirit abandons itself to its own movement, when effort fades into lazy condescension, when thought is engendered in its very flow.

A lot of what is visible to us of the way Borges approached his passion for language and literature, has to do with this "maturity of intelligence", something he received as a teaching from his father. To read whatever he enjoyed, to read for pleasure, and to write when the inspiration came, and not to rush to publish. Such beautiful privilege makes for the concentrated wine, the slow and easy ebb, of Borges' stories, and his reflections on literature.

Borges shared with us Herbert Spencer's idea that teaching grammar is a mistake. Spencer, according to Borges, thought that grammar was the "philosophy of language," and so it is unnecessary to study it. It can be studied later on. Besides, he added, no child learns their language through grammar.

We can add to Borges' remarks regarding Spencer's ideas that any experienced language teacher with some sense will tell you that nobody learns through grammar rules. You learn through authentic and comprehensible interaction.

Concerning the learning process, William James wrote in *Pragmatism: A New Name for Some Old Ways of Thinking*:

The novelty soaks in; it stains the ancient mass; but it is also tinged by what absorbs it. Our past apperceives and co-operates; and in the new equilibrium in which each step forward in the process of learning terminates, it happens relatively seldom that the new fact is added RAW. More usually it is embedded cooked, as one might say, or stewed down in the sauce of the old.

The question is, what does the "ancient mass" consist of when learning to speak your language? If one is learning naturally, as a native speaker, then it occurs through your interaction with a world. Through every little thing and person. This explains also why, although a child can learn a basic level of fluent communication by the time they are four years old, many people who learn through the old school, strictly grammatical route may learn how to decipher textbook sentences but cannot communicate efficiently in the target language even after a decade. Immersion is needed, and it is context that gives things their proper place for the brain to utilize.

Further, in the first volume of *The Principles of Psychology*, William James writes:

In kindergarten instruction one of the exercises is to make the children see how many features they can point out in such an object as a flower or a stuffed bird. They readily name the features they know already, such as leaves, tail, bill, feet. But they may look for hours without distinguishing nostrils, claws, scales, etc., until their attention is called to these details; thereafter, however, they see them every time. In short, the only things which we commonly see are those which we preperceive. and the only things which we preperceive are those which have been labelled for us, and the labels stamped into our mind. If we lost our stock of labels we should be intellectually lost in the midst of the world.

In other words, we proceed by identifying things and having them become part of our experience. And this is a fact that is capitalized on in the classroom. For someone like Borges, who learned just enough of certain languages to make his way through books, the old grammatical way must have sufficed. He did not need a teacher to point at vegetables and tell him what they were. He did not need to be told about the words used in conveying day-to-day feelings, either. He needed just enough German in context to understand the poetry of Heine, of Goethe, and so on.

By his own admission, Borges was not a great speaker of languages. That was not his interest. His interest was in literature, in the art of writing, in the world of letters, and he had the sense, the instinct, to adhere to his desires. Even when speaking in English, we can tell he has a very refined sense of grammar, yet an almost undecipherable (at first) accent that can seem unbearable to most native speakers. No matter.

What is most interesting is that even someone as bookish and library-bound person such as Borges, it was clear that one had to learn the language naturally. It is also true that he learned German from the poetry of Heine, and not from memorizing grammar rules. He has the experience, then, and also the sense, for he was, if anything, a man of keen common sense, to signal that all language learning had to proceed from an engagement with the authentic experience.

Herbert Spencer himself writes in *Essays on Education and Kindred Subjects*:

Observe next, that this formal instruction, far too soon commenced, is carried on with but little reference to the laws of mental development. Intellectual progress is of necessity from the concrete to the abstract. But regardless of this, highly abstract studies, such as grammar, which should come quite late, are begun quite early. Political geography, dead and uninteresting to a child, and which should be an appendage of sociological studies, is commenced betimes; while physical geography, comprehensible and comparatively attractive to a child, is in great part passed over.

And this is true of language learning, too. We are brought into a classroom. Suddenly, we are taught the most pedestrian rudiments of it, in the sense that they are not interesting nor stimulating, and then we are constantly bombarded with grammar rules and word banks.

What made Borges such a great consumer and absolute lover of *certain* German literature was the fact that, from the beginning, he made it a point to go after what he loved. It was most important for him to understand the words and the phrases so that he could taste of the poetry, so that he could dive into the world of the artist. To him, every moment spent with the new language was an adventure.

Angelus Silesius writes the following verses:
Rein wie das feinste Gold, steif wie ein Felsenstein,
Ganz lauter wie Kristall, soll dein Gemüte sein.

Which roughly translate as:
Pure as the finest gold, stiff as a rock,
Your mind should be as loud as crystal.

The first line tells us, if one may venture an interpretation, of only letting through the best, and to be firm in this. The last conveys something of a vibratory quality. The idea of being "in tune" or "in the same frequency" with certain things, and not with others. The decision to alight upon certain pastures but to pass over others as "not quite right". The decision, to go down abandoned paths because they shine with the light of a fire that we recognize as our own.

The natural, the organic

At a certain point during Borges' first interview in the Spanish literature television program *A Fondo*, the interviewer comments on conversations having their characteristic twists and turns. Borges answers that if it were not this way, they would not be alive, that they must branch out.

In a poem titled "The Human Abstract," William Blake talks about a great tree. Its branches extend a mystery over those who sit under it. Its fruits are sweet and full of deceit. The gods of the earth and the see, Blake tells us, have searched in vain for this tree within nature. The final line of the poem tells us that said tree grows inside the human brain.

Even though it may seem spectacular, we coincide with Chesterton's opinion in his book dedicated to Blake:
There was nothing of the obviously fervid and futile about Blake's supernaturalism. It was not his frenzy but his coolness that was startling.

We hear from Chesterton that Blake did not say these things in a superfluous manner, nor on a whim. He tells us that what really surprises us about Blake is that serenity with which he tells us these things. It is that same serenity, that way of taking things and reducing them to a common sense, of letting things take their natural course with an attitude of observation, which was also very characteristic of Borges.

Borges said he did not like Wagner because he had made everything too romantic, too emphatic. That Wagner had not understood the Scandinavian. "Or," Borges added, in his typical way of hedging his opinions, "it may be that I do not understand Wagner, or both things. I ignore as much about Wagner as he ignored about the essentially Scandinavian."

In other words, Wagner had instilled stiffness and choked out the life out of the Scandinavian myth. To fully understand Borges' posture, we must understand what he saw in the ancient Teutonic-Scandinavian stories. He wrote once, in his *Nueve ensayos dantescos*, that the Scandinavian feels secret, as if one were in a dream.

Borges does not tell us exactly how he believes Wagner interpreted the Scandinavian, or rather how he misinterpreted it. George Bernard Shaw tells us that in Wagner's *The Ring of the Nibelungs* everything is grandiose and solemn. If we take both observations to heart, we realize that what Shaw describes regarding Wagner's work contrasts greatly with what Borges described about the original material, the spirit of the Scandinavian.

Victor Rydberg, in his magnum opus *Undersökningar i germanisk mythologi* (*Investigations in German Mythology*), refers to the circumstance and origin of Nordic stories as if they were memories and imaginations full of intrigues and secrets. We constantly see characters changing bodies or shape, giving different names for themselves and to others. Decisions taken center entirely in the momentary feeling of the character in each moment and make no reference to a higher or moral authority.

They bow down to nothing.

All of this coincides more with the individualist and anarchist vision of Borges than with the ideal of purity, greatness and pomp of Wagner, which the German Nationalists were later to take to extremes. Such extremes, we could observe, mean the death of the flowing vital essence that makes things conscious. The moment rigidity is imposed, you are left, at best, with a mechanical automaton following a programming.

Borges rather admired the toned down, clear-as-day, writings coming from Chinese culture, Taoism, Chinese and Japanese poetry. He described it as a desire to give everything, a fragrance, to give many things in a few necessary words. He called what they had taught the rest of us a *synthesis*.

Borges said on the matter, "A literature that believes in the possibility that a man say everything in a few casual words, that are not casual, of course. Reading Confucius one realizes that he has deliberately renounced to being rhetoric or pathetic. The fact of being sober, of being concise, of saying everything with a minimum of words, with a minimum of expression, with a minimum of emphasis. It strikes me as pretty. For I, who tend to be emphatic, it is a lesson. But what shall we do?"

About the Publisher

Totalitarian literature of Ascension.

Milton Keynes UK
Ingram Content Group UK Ltd.
UKHW042003281024
450365UK00003B/132